Hyperion, Isabella, The Eve of St. Agnes, [and] Lamia; Edited by G.E. Hollingworth

KEATS

HYPERION, ISABELLA
THE EVE OF ST. AGNES
LAMIA

EDITED BY

G. E. HOLLINGWORTH, M.A. Lond.

AUTHOR OF "A PRIMER OF LITERARY CRITICISM"
EDITOR OF ARNOLD: SOHRAB AND RUSTUM, THE SCHOLAR GIPSY, THYRSIS

London : W. B. CLIVE

University Tutorial Press Ld.

HIGH ST., NEW OXFORD ST., W.C.

PR
4832
H599

PRINTED IN GREAT BRITAIN BY UNIVERSITY TUTORIAL PRESS LD., AT THE
BURLINGTON PRESS, FOXTON, NEAR CAMBRIDGE

CONTENTS.

INTRODUCTION.

Keats's Life.—John Keats (b. 1795), like many other great writers, came of an undistinguished family : his father, a stableman, married his master's daughter ; and John, the first child, was born in the mews at Moorfields. Since his father was perhaps of Cornish descent, it is possible that in Keats, as in many other English poets, there was a Celtic strain. John, and later his brothers George and Tom, attended the school of the Rev. John Clarke at Enfield, where he received a sound general education, though he did not show any exceptional talent except for fighting boys bigger than himself—not, like the heroes of school-tales, in chivalrous defence of bullied weaklings, but from sheer quarrelsomeness.

In the last eighteen months of his school life, however, he turned studious, read at meal-times, did holiday tasks, devoured dictionaries of classical mythology, and became friendly with Charles Cowden Clarke, his schoolmaster's son, who afterwards became a literary man of some standing and who continued to foster Keats's love of poetry after the boy left school. This he did at the age of fifteen, his father and his mother being then both dead—the mother, of consumption. Keats was apprenticed to a surgeon, but left him before the close of the apprenticeship, and took to walking St. Thomas's Hospital ; he passed the usual examination in 1815, and became a dresser at Guy's Hospital.

But his heart had never been in his work ; in 1812 he had borrowed Spenser's *Faery Queene* from Cowden Clarke, read it all with the utmost enthusiasm, and became more and more determined to be a poet. Through Cowden

Clarke he had come to know Leigh Hunt, the essayist, critic, and poet, editor of *The Examiner*, who had recently served two years' imprisonment for referring to the Prince Regent as a fat Adonis of forty. Probably in the youthful eyes of Keats this charming champion of liberty was a hero ; certainly he had a great influence, not always good, upon Keats's early poetry. Through Hunt, too, Keats became acquainted with Haydon, the noble-minded but unpractical painter of very large historical pictures, with Reynolds, a poet now forgotten, and with Ollier, the publisher, who in 1817 issued Keats's first volume of poems. In 1817, too, and the next year, Keats visited the Isle of Wight, Margate, Oxford, Stratford-on-Avon, Leatherhead, Dorking, and Teignmouth, returning to Hampstead, his permanent quarters, at intervals, and busying himself with the writing of *Endymion*, for which he had already found a publisher willing to advance a considerable sum on account. It will be seen, then, that Keats, so far from being a cockney poet in mean circumstances, had passed a good part of his time in the country, and had found his private fortune sufficient to provide for him comfortably while he made his first essays in poetry.

In April 1818 *Endymion* was published, and two months later Keats set off on a pedestrian tour with a friend, Charles Armitage Brown, starting from Liverpool, where they had seen George Keats off to settle in America, and travelling through the Lake country, the Burns country, Belfast, and the Western Highlands. Keats, with his customary energy and ardour—an energy and ardour too often characteristic of incipient consumption—frequently walked twenty miles or more a day and "roughed it" in a way most unwise for one whose health had already given cause for anxiety. In Scotland, however, after wading through miles of bog, and trying in vain to throw off the resulting chill, he gave up the tour and returned home— only to find his brother Tom dying of consumption. For three months Keats nursed his brother devotedly, thereby probably sealing his own fate.

After the death of Tom, he set up house with Armitage Brown at Hampstead, and divided his attention between poetry and love for a Miss Brawne. He became engaged, but found no happiness: his sensitiveness made him absurdly angry at the rather tasteless chaff of his friends ; his gathering ill-health increased his irritability. Miss Brawne, who was five years his junior, appears to have been a perfectly normal girl, light-hearted and perhaps occasionally inclined to tease, but genuinely attached to him, though incapable of his own fierce passion. The poet was jealous and unhappy ; sure that he neither deserved nor had her love ; angry that she did not (as he thought) give it.

His misery and the excitement aroused by the reception of *Endymion*—which was most scurrilously assailed in *The Quarterly Review* and *Blackwood's Magazine* by the political opponents of Hunt—probably hastened his death , but it is as untrue to say that he was killed by his critics as to say that he died of love. He had a serious breakdown in February 1820 and, though he rallied, it was only for a few months.

In September 1820 he left for Italy in the company of Severn, a student-painter. Shelley, then at Pisa, invited him to go there ; but since he had a letter of introduction to Dr. Clark in Rome, Keats settled in the latter town under the devoted care of Severn. The poet knew that he was living what he called a " posthumous life," and felt bitterly that he was dying with fame just beyond his grasp.

After some months of agonising illness, he died, aged twenty-five. He was buried in the English cemetery at Rome, and upon his tombstone were inscribed, at his own request, the words *Here lies one whose name was writ in water.*

Keats's Character and Aims.—The last year, at least, of Keats's life was so devastated by illness that little of his natural character remained : we have thus merely a short twenty-four years, of which only some three or four have left any detailed record. Yet, despite the immaturity inevitable in so young a man, Keats's character leaves a singularly vivid and consistent impression.

He was a man peculiarly sensitive to all the pleasures and beauties which the material world can offer : he found an exquisite delight in fine tastes, in graceful or noble forms, in light, in colour, in sound, in physical exertion. His love of a meadow was not, like Wordsworth's, a communion with the spirit of Nature : it was a childlike joy in the coolness, the softness, the greenness of grass, in the hot sun and the blue sky—primarily an animal rather than a spiritual enjoyment. There is a story that he sprinkled his throat with cayenne so as to enjoy the better by contrast the delicious coolness of claret. It may or may not be true ; but it is admirably characteristic of Keats with his impetuosity, his love of sensations, his rather morbid willingness to suffer present discomfort for the sake of heightening future pleasure.

Clearly such a nature might turn easily to the life of the sybarite, but from this Keats was saved by a delight equally intense in the morally and intellectually beautiful. He was as keenly alive to the fineness of a noble deed or of a phrase flashing with genius as to the fineness of the first white flower against the black branches and the cloudy March sky. For him beauty was " a joy for ever," a spirit enduring even after the destruction of the forms in which it expressed itself. Man himself might " sink into nothingness "—Keats had no sure belief in immortality and was morbidly obsessed by the thought of death—but the beauty of the nightingale's song, of an old legend, of a Grecian urn would remain for ever : in a world of transition, unrest, impermanence and illusion, beauty alone was calm, unchanging, permanent, real. In his own words :—

> " Beauty is truth, truth beauty "—that is all
> Ye know on earth, and all ye need to know.

Yet, dowered as Keats was with all the sensibility of the poet, he yet had all the sense of the practical business-man He is totally unlike the wild-eyed, dreamy poet of popular imagination, who seizes a pen in an ecstasy of inspiration and writes without a blot immortal words of complete originality. Inspiration he had in plenty ; but he supplemented it by the most diligent study and the most severe self-criticism. He set himself deliberately to learn and copy the best effects of the best masters in his craft ; he polished and repolished his verses, and some of his most famous phrases were painfully evolved, after repeated alteration, from an originally commonplace line.

The discipline which he brought to bear upon his verse he brought to bear also upon his own character. Since a poet feels more widely and more intensely than the common man, he is necessarily a man of strong and varied emotions, of changing moods and unstable outlook. The peculiar danger of his temperament is that he may let his moods be his masters instead of his servants ; treat all of them as of equal value and become a mere weathercock turned idly by whatever neurotic breeze may blow. Keats was alive to his danger ; instead of letting himself be overwhelmed with anger or despair at the cruel reception of *Endymion*, he summoned up all his fortitude and went on writing, profiting by every grain of truth in the hostile criticism.

Even when his brother was dying and he was himself full of premonitory fears of his own death, he still worked on steadily, not writing wild laments at his hard fate, but laboriously fashioning poems characterised by a restraint and self-mastery remarkable in anyone so young, more remarkable still in anyone so ardent, and most remarkable of all in one living as he did at a time when restraint was considered a fault. Keats's rule of life is summed up in the words of his own Oceanus :—

> To bear all naked truths,
> And to envisage circumstance, all calm,
> That is the top of sovereignty.

Keats's Age.—This was a strange doctrine in the age of
Byron and Shelley, who questioned all established codes of
conduct, all conventions and all institutions. Byron's
heroes, drawn from himself, or what he imagined himself
to be, were lawless, dark, passionate, stained with
mysterious crimes, flashing in a moment from gentleness
into fury. Shelley's heroes, more noble, preached that
man himself was inherently good, that all vices sprang
from repression and that a world in which there was no
law but love would be perfect. Leigh Hunt, Keats's early
guide and the intimate friend of Shelley, was another
apostle of freedom : most of Keats's literary circle held in
greater or less degree the same views. It says much for
Keats's essential sanity that he, while sharing their love of
freedom and hatred of tyranny, yet avoided the excesses
into which they were led by the ardour of their resistance to
the oppression, cant, and convention which characterised
their time.

The contrast is equally marked in literary ideals and
methods. Keats, like all the great poets of his time,
belonged to the Romantic school, the school which,
following Coleridge and Wordsworth, had revolted against
the artificial and townish Classicism of the school of Pope.
Pope had written heroic couplets, neatly divided into halves
and stopped at the end : he had loved witty maxims and
a man-of-the-world air : his own ideal he expressed in the
words—

> True wit is nature to advantage dressed,
> What oft was thought, but ne'er so well expressed.

The Romantic school hated all that Pope loved : it loved
Nature undressed, and preferred new thoughts to old : it
disliked and distrusted Pope's cold reasoning ; it preferred
hot feeling.

Keats shared to the full this revolt against artificiality.
In one of his early poems, *Sleep and Poetry*, he refers
contemptuously to Classicism as " a schism nurtured by
foppery and barbarism . . . a school of dolts"; his dislike

of the coldly analytic type of reasoning is evident in his famous cry that science has tarnished the beauty of the rainbow—

> We know its woof, its texture : it is given
> In the dull catalogue of common things.

The same distrust of the matter-of-fact of the materialist inspires his *Lamia,* and is the real interpretation of the ejaculation in one of his letters : " O, for a life of sensations rather than of thoughts "—that is, a life of intuition, guided by the highest of our feelings, rather than a life lived by rule and devoted to purely mental activity.

The Classical Element in Keats.—But if Keats was a Romantic, he was also a Classicist, not as Pope's school understood the word, but in the sense that he had much of the spirit of the old Greeks—a desire for a perfected rather than an adumbrated beauty, a delight in finished workmanship rather than in vague suggestiveness, a feeling for form. Added to this were a deep interest in the subject-matter of the old Greek writers—the myths of gods and titans, nymphs and fauns—and that innocent pagan delight in the physical side of life already remarked. Perhaps none of our poets has been so Greek as this lad, who never saw Greece and did not read Greek.

It was this Greek strain in Keats, we may suppose, which made him discard the literary excesses of his early models and which showed him the merits even of the despised Classical school. The history of Keats's works, indeed, is the history of a series of experiments : Keats was willing to learn from any poet who had anything to teach.

Keats's Works and Models.—The two influences most apparent in his first volume, *Poems* (1817) are those of Spenser and Leigh Hunt. Though the volume shows promise, it cannot be said to achieve much. *Endymion* is on a different level and, though it has serious defects, the poetic ability evident in it is so great that there is no excuse for the severity of the attacks made upon it by *The Quarterly Review* and *Blackwood's*. It is an allegorical tale of Endymion's love for the goddess of the Moon, a tale certainly very confused and rambling, but full of fine poetic passages. Keats's model was still Spenser, and Spenser had little notion of how to tell a story in a clear and interesting manner.

Moreover, the evil influence of Leigh Hunt is again evident. Keats owed a great debt to Leigh Hunt for his encouragement, for his fine critical acumen, for the talk and the reading to which he introduced him, perhaps for something of the easy narrative which he later developed and which is one of Hunt's chief poetic merits. But there was a streak of vulgarity in Hunt which had led his enemies to dub him and his colleagues and imitators "the Cockney School." He was inclined to smack his lips too vigorously over anything he liked ; to write gushing or over-luscious descriptions , to drop from tragedy into tasteless jocosity under the impression that he was thus giving his verse realism and contact with everyday life. Keats's taste was unformed, and there was always a feverish and unbalanced strain in his nature—a strain which, by his own stern self-discipline, he almost eliminated later, but which came out vividly again in his letters to Fanny Brawne, when illness had broken down his self-control. This strain was greatly accentuated by Hunt's influence.

But it was not the defects of *Endymion,* whether due to Spenser's or Hunt's influence or to Keats's own immaturity, which led to the scurrilous attacks of the reviews : it was the fact that he was known to be a friend of Hunt. And though, as we have seen, the reviews did not kill him, they undoubtedly embittered his death. For they had effectually prevented him from gaining in his lifetime that fame which he so earnestly desired · he was confident that had he lived he would have achieved fame in spite of his detractors : he was equally sure that, dying as he did, he would be forgotten. It is difficult to decide upon which side of the account with Leigh Hunt the balance lies.

From *Endymion* Keats turned to the poems contained in this volume : *Lamia, Isabella, The Eve of St. Agnes, and other Poems* was published in 1820, when Keats was already very seriously ill. Besides *Hyperion* the " other poems " included much of Keats's very finest work—*To Autumn, The Ode on a Grecian Urn, The Ode to a Nightingale, The Ode to Psyche,* and *The Ode on Melancholy.* Except for this volume and an odd poem or so in magazines, nothing more was published till after his death, and little more was written. Most of his other work collected and published posthumously was itself written during the wonderful two years, 1818-19, which saw the composition of this volume.

Of these other poems the most important are a recast of the beginning of *Hyperion,* fine in patches, but on the whole inferior to the first attempt, *La Belle Dame Sans Merci* ; *The Eve of St. Mark* ; the tragedy of *Otho the Great,* for which Armitage Brown provided the whole invention of the first four acts, Keats inventing the fifth act but merely versifying the others ; the trivial frivolity of *The Cap and Bells* ; and the best of the sonnets.

The bulk, the variety, and the high general level of excellence of the output of these two years is astonishing. Given but another ten years of healthy life as full of progress and achievement, Keats might have outshone every other poet in the history of English literature. All young poets are imitative ; but none has been so successfully imitative and original at the same time as Keats.

He read Chaucer, and learnt from him the easy narrative, the mastery of the octave, and the natural pathos of *Isabella,* and the mediaeval atmosphere of *The Eve of St. Agnes* ; he read Milton and learnt the sublimity of reverberant blank verse, the " large utterance of the early gods," the titanic conceptions of *Hyperion* ; he read Chatterton and Coleridge and learnt the eerie magic of *La Belle Dame* ; most amazing of all, he, the Romantic and friend of Romantics, read Dryden, the great first head of the hated Classical school, and, abandoning the looseness of his

Endymion couplets, learnt how to marry in *Lamia* all the
ease and clearness and restraint of the Restoration heroic
couplet with all the splendour of imaginative feeling of the
Romantics.

Of course he made mistakes : not all his borrowings are
good. The execrable taste of the opening of Part II. of
Lamia is due to imitation of Dryden's Restoration levity
and cynicism—a levity and cynicism in admirable keeping
with Dryden's subjects, but hopelessly incongruous in a
poem whose whole success depends upon regarding love
seriously. And sometimes his borrowing itself is unsuccess-
ful : his sonnets at their best occasionally have a hint of
Shakespeare, but his attempt at a Shakespearean tragedy
in *Otho the Great* was bound to fail. So, too, if *The Cap
and Bells* is indeed intended to imitate Ariosto, it is a
miserably poor copy.

But Keats himself was in general the first to discover
his own defects and the first to see how to remedy them.
He deliberately chose Milton as a corrective to his lack of
restraint ; he as deliberately abandoned *Hyperion* when he
discovered that it was becoming " too Miltonic," and that
his own natural style was in danger of being submerged.

For, despite all his imitation, Keats is always individual.
Even in *Hyperion,* where he " copies " most closely, there
are no two lines which Milton could have written. It is
difficult to define Keats's own style—easy to feel it. It is
not a mere matter of favourite tricks of phrase, though
Keats has many—pet words like *silver, pale, nest, convulsed,
swoon, lush* ; a fondness for compound words, for new
adverbial formations such as *refreshfully* and *palely,* a
habit of treating the *-ed* of the past tense of verbs as a
separate syllable—indeed, most of Keats's favourite words
have been industriously traced to Chaucer or Spenser,
Chapman or Massinger, Milton or Chatterton, or some other
of the many elder poets whose works Keats studied so
eagerly.

Perhaps, as in all good styles, the individuality is as much
a matter of outlook and feeling as of words. Keats may

borrow Milton's grand style, but he keeps his own eager eye, his own young and entirely unpuritan delight in the senses, his own glowing imagination : Milton could never have written :—

> Voiceless, or hoarse with loud *tormented* streams

or

> a few stars
> Were lingering in the heavens, while the thrush
> Began calm-throated.

And in the great *Odes*, where Keats's own philosophy of life finds its supreme expression, his style shakes itself free from reminiscence and echo and becomes no longer Milton suffused with Keats or Keats flushed with Spenser, but pure Keats—the authoritative note of a great and original genius.

HYPERION.

BOOK I.

DEEP in the shady sadness of a vale
Far sunken from the healthy breath of morn,
Far from the fiery noon, and eve's one star,
Sat gray-hair'd Saturn. quiet as a stone,
Still as the silence round about his lair ;   5
Forest on forest hung about his head
Like cloud on cloud.   No stir of air was there,
Not so much life as on a summer's day
Robs not one light seed from the feather'd grass,
But where the dead leaf fell, there did it rest.   10
A stream went voiceless by, still deadened more
By reason of his fallen divinity
Spreading a shade : the Naiad 'mid her reeds
Press'd her cold finger closer to her lips.

Along the margin-sand large foot-marks went,   15
No further than to where his feet had stray'd,
And slept there since.   Upon the sodden ground
His old right hand lay nerveless, listless, dead,
Unsceptred ; and his realmless eyes were closed ;
While his bow'd head seem'd list'ning to the Earth, 20
His ancient mother, for some comfort yet.

It seem'd no force could wake him from his place ;
But there came one, who with a kindred hand

Touch'd his wide shoulders, after bending low
With reverence, though to one who knew it not.   25
She was a Goddess of the infant world ;
By her in stature the tall Amazon
Had stood a pigmy's height : she would have ta'en
Achilles by the hair and bent his neck ;
Or with a finger stay'd Ixion's wheel.   30
Her face was large as that of Memphian sphinx,
Pedestal'd haply in a palace court,
When sages look'd to Egypt for their lore.
But oh ! how unlike marble was that face :
How beautiful, if sorrow had not made   35
Sorrow more beautiful than Beauty's self.
There was a listening fear in her regard,
As if calamity had but begun ;
As if the vanward clouds of evil days
Had spent their malice, and the sullen rear   40
Was with its stored thunder labouring up.
One hand she press'd upon that aching spot
Where beats the human heart, as if just there,
Though an immortal, she felt cruel pain :
The other upon Saturn's bended neck   45
She laid, and to the level of his ear
Leaning with parted lips, some words she spake
In solemn tenour and deep organ tone :
Some mourning words, which in our feeble tongue
Would come in these like accents ; O how frail   50
To that large utterance of the early Gods !
" Saturn, look up !—though wherefore, poor old King ?
I have no comfort for thee, no not one :
I cannot say, ' O wherefore sleepest thou ? '
For heaven is parted from thee, and the earth   55
Knows thee not, thus afflicted, for a God ;
And ocean too, with all its solemn noise,
Has from thy sceptre pass'd ; and all the air

Is emptied of thine hoary majesty.
Thy thunder, conscious of the new command, 60
Rumbles reluctant o'er our fallen house ;
And thy sharp lightning in unpractis'd hands
Scorches and burns our once serene domain.
O aching time !   O moments big as years !
All as ye pass swell out the monstrous truth, 65
And press it so upon our weary griefs
That unbelief has not a space to breathe.
Saturn, sleep on :—O thoughtless, why did I
Thus violate thy slumbrous solitude ?
Why should I ope thy melancholy eyes ? 70
Saturn, sleep on ! while at thy feet I weep."

  As when, upon a tranced summer-night,
Those green-rob'd senators of mighty woods,
Tall oaks, branch-charmed by the earnest stars,
Dream, and so dream all night without a stir, 75
Save from one gradual solitary gust
Which comes upon the silence, and dies off,
As if the ebbing air had but one wave ;
So came these words and went ; the while in tears
She touch'd her fair large forehead to the ground, 80
Just where her falling hair might be outspread
A soft and silken mat for Saturn's feet.
One moon, with alteration slow, had shed
Her silver seasons four upon the night,
And still these two were postured motionless, 85
Like natural sculpture in cathedral cavern ;
The frozen God still couchant on the earth,
And the sad Goddess weeping at his feet :
Until at length old Saturn lifted up
His faded eyes, and saw his kingdom gone, 90
And all the gloom and sorrow of the place,
And that fair kneeling Goddess ; and then spake,

As with a palsied tongue, and while his beard
Shook horrid with such aspen-malady :
" O tender spouse of gold Hyperion,   95
Thea, I feel thee ere I see thy face ;
Look up, and let me see our doom in it ;
Look up, and tell me if this feeble shape
Is Saturn's ; tell me, if thou hear'st the voice
Of Saturn ; tell me, if this wrinkling brow,   100
Naked and bare of its great diadem,
Peers like the front of Saturn.   Who had power
To make me desolate ? whence came the strength ?
How was it nurtur'd to such bursting forth,
While Fate seem'd strangled in my nervous grasp ? 105
But it is so ; and I am smother'd up,
And buried from all godlike exercise
Of influence benign on planets pale,
Of admonitions to the winds and seas,
Of peaceful sway above man's harvesting,   110
And all those acts which Deity supreme
Doth ease its heart of love in.—I am gone
Away from my own bosom : I have left
My strong identity, my real self,
Somewhere between the throne, and where I sit   115
Here on this spot of earth.   Search, Thea, search !
Open thine eyes eterne, and sphere them round
Upon all space : space starr'd, and lorn of light ;
Space region'd with life-air ; and barren void ;
Spaces of fire, and all the yawn of hell.—   120
Search, Thea, search ! and tell me, if thou seest
A certain shape or shadow, making way
With wings of chariot fierce to repossess
A heaven he lost erewhile : it must—it must
Be of ripe progress—Saturn must be King.   125
Yes, there must be a golden victory ;
There must be Gods thrown down, and trumpets blown

Of triumph calm, and hymns of festival
Upon the gold clouds metropolitan,
Voices of soft proclaim, and silver stir   130
Of strings in hollow shells ; and there shall be
Beautiful things made new, for the surprise
Of the sky-children ; I will give command :
Thea ! Thea ! Thea ! where is Saturn ? ”

This passion lifted him upon his feet,   135
And made his hands to struggle in the air,
His Druid locks to shake and ooze with sweat,
His eyes to fever out, his voice to cease.
He stood, and heard not Thea’s sobbing deep ;
A little time, and then again he snatch’d   140
Utterance thus.—“ But cannot I create ?
Cannot I form ?   Cannot I fashion forth
Another world, another universe,
To overbear and crumble this to nought ?
Where is another chaos ? Where ? ”—That word   145
Found way unto Olympus, and made quake
The rebel three.—Thea was startled up,
And in her bearing was a sort of hope,
As thus she quick-voic’d spake, yet full of awe.

“ This cheers our fallen house : come to our friends,
O Saturn ! come away, and give them heart ;   151
I know the covert, for thence came I hither.”
Thus brief ; then with beseeching eyes she went
With backward footing through the shade a space :
He follow’d, and she turn’d to lead the way   155
Through aged boughs, that yielded like the mist
Which eagles cleave upmounting from their nest.

Meanwhile in other realms big tears were shed,
More sorrow like to this, and such like woe,
Too huge for mortal tongue or pen of scribe :   160

The Titans fierce, self-hid, or prison-bound,
Groan'd for the old allegiance one more,
And listen'd in sharp pain for Saturn's voice.
But one of the whole mammoth-brood still kept
His sov'reignty, and rule, and majesty ;—   165
Blazing Hyperion on his orbed fire
Still sat, still snuff'd the incense, teeming up
From man to the sun's God ; yet unsecure :
For as among us mortals omens drear
Fright and perplex, so also shuddered he—   170
Not at dog's howl, or gloom-bird's hated screech,
Or the familiar visiting of one
Upon the first toll of his passing-bell,
Or prophesyings of the midnight lamp ;
But horrors, portion'd to a giant nerve,   175
Oft made Hyperion ache. His palace bright
Bastion'd with pyramids of glowing gold,
And touch'd with shade of bronzed obelisks,
Glar'd a blood-red through all its thousand courts,
Arches, and domes, and fiery galleries ;   180
And all its curtains of Aurorian clouds
Flush'd angerly : while sometimes eagle's wings,
Unseen before by Gods or wondering men,
Darken'd the place ; and neighing steeds were heard,
Not heard before by Gods or wondering men.   185
Also, when he would taste the spicy wreaths
Of incense, breath'd aloft from sacred hills,
Instead of sweets, his ample palate took
Savour of poisonous brass and metal sick :
And so, when harbour'd in the sleepy west,   190
After the full completion of fair day,—
For rest divine upon exalted couch
And slumber in the arms of melody,
He pac'd away the pleasant hours of ease
With stride colossal, on from hall to hall ;   195

While far within each aisle and deep recess,
His winged minions in close clusters stood,
Amaz'd and full of fear ; like anxious men
Who on wide plains gather in panting troops,
When earthquakes jar their battlements and towers.
Even now, while Saturn, rous'd from icy trance,   201
Went step for step with Thea through the woods,
Hyperion, leaving twilight in the rear,
Came slope upon the threshold of the west ,
Then, as was wont, his palace-door flew ope   205
In smoothest silence, save what solemn tubes,
Blown by the serious Zephyrs, gave of sweet
And wandering sounds, slow-breathed melodies ;
And like a rose in vermeil tint and shape,
In fragrance soft, and coolness to the eye,   210
That inlet to severe magnificence
Stood full blown, for the God to enter in.

   He enter'd, but he enter'd full of wrath ;
His flaming robes stream'd out beyond his heels,
And gave a roar, as if of earthly fire,   215
That scar'd away the meek ethereal Hours
And made their dove-wings tremble.   On he flared,
From stately nave to nave, from vault to vault,
Through bowers of fragrant and enwreathed light,
And diamond-paved lustrous long arcades,   220
Until he reach'd the great main cupola ;
There standing fierce beneath, he stamped his foot,
And from the basements deep to the high towers
Jarr'd his own golden region ; and before
The quavering thunder thereupon had ceas'd,   225
His voice leapt out, despite of godlike curb,
To this result : " O dreams of day and night !
O monstrous forms !   O effigies of pain !
O spectres busy in a cold, cold gloom !

O lank-ear'd Phantoms of black-weeded pools !   230
Why do I know ye ? why have I seen ye ? why
Is my eternal essence thus distraught
To see and to behold these horrors new ?
Saturn is fallen, am I too to fall ?
Am I to leave this haven of my rest,   235
This cradle of my glory, this soft clime,
This calm luxuriance of blissful light,
These crystalline pavilions, and pure fanes,
Of all my lucent empire ?   It is left
Deserted, void, nor any haunt of mine.   240
The blaze, the splendour, and the symmetry,
I cannot see—but darkness, death and darkness.
Even here, into my centre of repose,
The shady visions come to domineer,
Insult, and blind, and stifle up my pomp.—   245
Fall !—No, by Tellus and her briny robes !
Over the fiery frontier of my realms
I will advance a terrible right arm
Shall scare that infant thunderer, rebel Jove,
And bid old Saturn take his throne again."—   250
He spake, and ceas'd, the while a heavier threat
Held struggle with his throat but came not forth ;
For as in theatres of crowded men
Hubbub increases more they call out " Hush ! "
So at Hyperion's words the Phantoms pale   255
Bestirr'd themselves, thrice horrible and cold ;
And from the mirror'd level where he stood
A mist arose, as from a scummy marsh.
At this, through all his bulk an agony
Crept gradual, from the feet unto the crown,   260
Like a lithe serpent vast and muscular
Making slow way, with head and neck convuls'd
From over-strained might.   Releas'd, he fled
To the eastern gates, and full six dewy hours

Before the dawn in season due should blush,   265
He breath'd fierce breath against the sleepy portals,
Clear'd them of heavy vapours, burst them wide
Suddenly on the ocean's chilly streams.
The planet orb of fire, whereon he rode
Each day from east to west the heavens through, 270
Spun round in sable curtaining of clouds ;
Nor therefore veiled quiet, blindfold, and hid,
But ever and anon the glancing spheres,
Circles, and arcs, and broad-belting colure,
Glow'd through, and wrought upon the muffling dark
Sweet-shaped lightnings from the nadir deep   276
Up to the zenith,—hieroglyphics old
Which sages and keen-ey'd astrologers
Then living on the earth, with labouring thought
Won from the gaze of many centuries :   280
Now lost, save what we find on remnants huge
Of stone, or marble swart ; their import gone,
Their wisdom long since fled.—Two wings this orb
Possess'd for glory, two fair argent wings,
Ever exalted at the God's approach :   285
And now, from forth the gloom their plumes immense
Rose, one by one, till all outspreaded were ;
While still the dazzling globe maintain'd eclipse,
Awaiting for Hyperion's command.
Fain would he have commanded, fain took throne 290
And bid the day begin, if but for change.
He might not .—No, though a primeval God :
The sacred seasons might not be disturb'd.
Therefore the operations of the dawn
Stay'd in their birth, even as here 'tis told.   295
Those silver wings expanded sisterly,
Eager to sail their orb ; the porches wide
Open'd upon the dusk demesnes of night ;
And the bright Titan, phrenzied with new woes,

Unus'd to bend, by hard compulsion bent   300
His spirit to the sorrow of the time;
And all along a dismal rack of clouds,
Upon the boundaries of day and night,
He stretch'd himself in grief and radiance faint.
There as he lay, the Heaven with its stars   305
Look'd down on him with pity, and the voice
Of Coelus, from the universal space,
Thus whisper'd low and solemn in his ear.
" O brightest of my children dear, earth-born
And sky-engendered, Son of Mysteries   310
All unrevealed even to the powers
Which met at thy creating; at whose joys
And palpitations sweet, and pleasures soft,
I, Coelus, wonder, how they came and whence;
And at the fruits thereof what shapes they be,   315
Distinct, and visible; symbols divine,
Manifestations of that beauteous life
Diffus'd unseen throughout eternal space :
Of these new-form'd art thou, oh brightest child !
Of these, thy brethren and the Goddesses !   320
There is sad feud among ye, and rebellion
Of son against his sire. I saw him fall,
I saw my first-born tumbled from the throne !
To me his arms were spread, to me his voice
Found way from forth the thunders round his head !
Pale wox I, and in vapours hid my face.   326
Art thou, too, near such doom ? vague fear there is :
For I have seen my sons most unlike Gods.
Divine ye were created, and divine
In sad demeanour, solemn, undisturb'd,   330
Unruffled, like high Gods, ye liv'd and ruled :
Now I behold in you fear, hope, and wrath ;
Actions of rage and passion ; even as
I see them, on the mortal world beneath,

In men who die.—This is the grief, O Son !   335
Sad sign of ruin, sudden dismay, and fall !
Yet do thou strive ; as thou art capable,
As thou canst move about, an evident God ;
And canst oppose to each malignant hour
Ethereal presence :—I am but a voice ;   340
My life is but the life of winds and tides,
No more than winds and tides can I avail —
But thou canst.—Be thou therefore in the van
Of circumstance ; yea, seize the arrow's barb
Before the tense string murmur.—To the earth !   345
For there thou wilt find Saturn, and his woes.
Meantime I will keep watch on thy bright sun,
And of thy seasons be a careful nurse."—
Ere half this region-whisper had come down,
Hyperion arose, and on the stars   350
Lifted his curved lids, and kept them wide
Until it ceas'd ; and still he kept them wide :
And still they were the same bright, patient stars.
Then with a slow incline of his broad breast,
Like to a diver in the pearly seas,   355
Forward he stoop'd over the airy shore,
And plung'd all noiseless into the deep night.

BOOK II.

Just at the self-same beat of Time's wide wings
Hyperion slid into the rustled air,
And Saturn gain'd with Thea that sad place
Where Cybele and the bruised Titans mourn'd.
It was a den where no insulting light   5
Could glimmer on their tears ; where their own groans
They felt, but heard not, for the solid roar
Of thunderous waterfalls and torrents hoarse,
Pouring a constant bulk, uncertain where.
Crag jutting forth to crag, and rocks that seem'd   10
Ever as if just rising from a sleep,
Forehead to forehead held their monstrous horns ;
And thus in thousand hugest phantasies
Made a fit roofing to this nest of woe.
Instead of thrones, hard flint they sat upon,   15
Couches of rugged stone, and slaty ridge
Stubborn'd with iron.   All were not assembled :
Some chain'd in torture, and some wandering.
Coeus, and Gyges, and Briareüs,
Typhon, and Dolor, and Porphyrion,   20
With many more, the brawniest in assault,
Were pent in regions of laborious breath ;
Dungeon'd in opaque element, to keep
Their clenched teeth still clench'd, and all their limbs
Lock'd up like veins of metal, crampt and screw'd ;   25
Without a motion, save of their big hearts
Heaving in pain, and horribly convuls'd

With sanguine feverous boiling gurge of pulse.
Mnemosyne was straying in the world ;
Far from her moon had Phoebe wandered ;　　　30
And many else were free to roam abroad,
But for the main, here found they covert drear.
Scarce images of life, one here, one there,
Lay vast and edgeways ; like a dismal cirque
Of Druid stones, upon a forlorn moor,　　　35
When the chill rain begins at shut of eve,
In dull November, and their chancel vault,
The Heaven itself, is blinded throughout night.
Each one kept shroud, nor to his neighbour gave
Or word, or look, or action of despair.　　　40
Creus was one ; his ponderous iron mace
Lay by him, and a shatter'd rib of rock
Told of his rage, ere he thus sank and pined.
Iápetus another ; in his grasp,
A serpent's plashy neck ; its barbed tongue　　45
Squeez'd from the gorge, and all its uncurl'd length
Dead ; and because the creature could not spit
Its poison in the eyes of conquering Jove.
Next Cottus : prone he lay, chin uppermost,
As though in pain ; for still upon the flint　　50
He ground severe his skull, with open mouth
And eyes at horrid working.　Nearest him
Asia, born of most enormous Caf,
Who cost her mother Tellus keener pangs,
Though feminine, than any of her sons :　　55
More thought than woe was in her dusky face,
For she was prophesying of her glory ;
And in her wide imagination stood
Palm-shaded temples, and high rival fanes,
By Oxus or in Ganges' sacred isles.　　　60
Even as hope upon her anchor leans,
So leant she, not so fair, upon a tusk

Shed from the broadest of her elephants.
Above her, on a crag's uneasy shelve,
Upon his elbow rais'd, all prostrate else,   65
Shadow'd Enceladus ; once tame and mild
As grazing ox unworried in the meads ;
Now tiger-passion'd, lion-thoughted, wroth,
He meditated, plotted, and even now
Was hurling mountains in that second war,   70
Not long delay'd, that scar'd the younger Gods
To hide themselves in forms of beast and bird.
Not far hence Atlas ; and beside him prone
Phorcus, the sire of Gorgons. Neighbour'd close
Oceanus, and Tethys, in whose lap   75
Sobb'd Clymene among her tangled hair.
In midst of all lay Themis, at the feet
Of Ops the queen all clouded round from sight ,
No shape distinguishable, more than when
Thick night confounds the pine-tops with the clouds :
And many else whose names may not be told.   81
For when the Muse's wings are air-ward spread,
Who shall delay her flight ?   And she must chaunt
Of Saturn, and his guide, who now had climb'd
With damp and slippery footing from a depth   85
More horrid still.   Above a sombre cliff
Their heads appear'd, and up their stature grew
Till on the level height their steps found ease :
Then Thea spread abroad her trembling arms
Upon the precincts of this nest of pain,   90
And sidelong fix'd her eye on Saturn's face :
There saw she direst strife ; the supreme God
At war with all the frailty of grief,
Of rage, of fear, anxiety, revenge,
Remorse, spleen, hope, but most of all despair.   95
Against these plagues he strove in vain ; for Fate
Had pour'd a mortal oil upon his head,

A disanointing poison : so that Thea,
Affrightened, kept her still, and let him pass
First onwards in, among the fallen tribe.   100

   As with us mortal men, the laden heart
Is persecuted more, and fever'd more,
When it is nighing to the mournful house
Where other hearts are sick of the same bruise ;
So Saturn, as he walk'd into the midst,   105
Felt faint, and would have sunk among the rest,
But that he met Enceladus's eye,
Whose mightiness, and awe of him, at once
Came like an inspiration ; and he shouted,
" Titans, behold your God ! " at which some groan'd ;
Some started on their feet ; some also shouted ;   111
Some wept, some wail'd, all bow'd with reverence ;
And Ops, uplifting her black folded veil,
Show'd her pale cheeks, and all her forehead wan,
Her eye-brows thin and jet, and hollow eyes.   115
There is a roaring in the bleak-grown pines
When winter lifts his voice ; there is a noise
Among immortals when a God gives sign,
With hushing finger, how he means to load
His tongue with the full weight of utterless thought, 120
With thunder, and with music, and with pomp :
Such noise is like the roar of bleak-grown pines :
Which, when it ceases in this mountain'd world,
No other sound succeeds ; but ceasing here,
Among these fallen, Saturn's voice therefrom   125
Grew up like organ, that begins anew
Its strain, when other harmonies, stopt short,
Leave the dinn'd air vibrating silverly.
Thus grew it up—" Not in my own sad breast,
Which is its own great judge and searcher out,   130
Can I find reason why ye should be thus :

Not in the legends of the first of days,
Studied from that old spirit-leaved book
Which starry Uranus with finger bright
Sav'd from the shores of darkness, when the waves   135
Low-ebb'd still hid it up in shallow gloom ;—
And the which book ye know I ever kept
For my first-based footstool :—Ah, infirm !
Not there, nor in sign, symbol, or portent
Of element, earth, water, air, and fire,—   140
At war, at peace, or inter-quarreling
One against one, or two, or three, or all
Each several one against the other three,
As fire with air loud warring when rain-floods
Drown both, and press them both against earth's face,
Where, finding sulphur, a quadruple wrath   146
Unhinges the poor world ;—not in that strife,
Wherefrom I take strange lore, and read it deep,
Can I find reason why ye should be thus :
No, no-where can unriddle, though I search,   150
And pore on Nature's universal scroll
Even to swooning, why ye, Divinities,
The first-born of all shap'd and palpable Gods,
Should cower beneath what, in comparison,
Is untremendous might.   Yet ye are here,   155
O'erwhelm'd, and spurn'd, and batter'd, ye are here !
O Titans, shall I say, ' Arise ! '—Ye groan :
Shall I say ' Crouch ! '—Ye groan.   What can I then ?
O Heaven wide !   O unseen parent dear !
What can I ?   Tell me, all ye brethren Gods,   160
How can we war, how engine our great wrath !
O speak your counsel now, for Saturn's ear
Is all a-hunger'd.   Thou, Oceanus,
Ponderest high and deep ; and in thy face
I see, astonied, that severe content   165
Which comes of thought and musing : give us help ! "

So ended Saturn ; and the God of the Sea,
Sophist and sage, from no Athenian grove,
But cogitation in his watery shades,
Arose, with locks not oozy, and began,   170
In murmurs, which his first-endeavouring tongue
Caught infant-like from the far-foamed sands.
" O ye, whom wrath consumes ! who, passion-stung,
Writhe at defeat, and nurse your agonies !
Shut up your senses, stifle up your ears,   175
My voice is not a bellows unto ire.
Yet listen, ye who will, whilst I bring proof
How ye, perforce, must be content to stoop :
And in the proof much comfort will I give,
If ye will take that comfort in its truth.   180
We fall by course of Nature's law, not force
Of thunder, or of Jove.   Great Saturn, thou
Hast sifted well the atom-universe ;
But for this reason, that thou art the King,
And only blind from sheer supremacy,   185
One avenue was shaded from thine eyes,
Through which I wandered to eternal truth.
And first, as thou wast not the first of powers,
So art thou not the last ; it cannot be :
Thou art not the beginning nor the end.   190
From chaos and parental darkness came
Light, the first fruits of that intestine broil,
That sullen ferment, which for wondrous ends
Was ripening in itself.   The ripe hour came,
And with it light, and light, engendering   195
Upon its own producer, forthwith touch'd
The whole enormous matter into life.
Upon that very hour, our parentage,
The Heavens and the Earth, were manifest :
Then thou first born, and we the giant race,   200
Found ourselves ruling new and beauteous realms.

KTS.   2

Now comes the pain of truth, to whom 'tis pain ,
O folly ! for to bear all naked truths,
And to envisage circumstance, all calm,
That is the top of sovereignty.   Mark well !   205
As Heaven and Earth are fairer, fairer far
Than Chaos and blank Darkness, though once chiefs ;
And as we show beyond that Heaven and Earth
In form and shape compact and beautiful,
In will, in action free, companionship,   210
And thousand other signs of purer life ;
So on our heels a fresh perfection treads,
A power more strong in beauty, born of us
And fated to excel us, as we pass
In glory that old Darkness : nor are we   215
Thereby more conquer'd, than by us the rule
Of shapeless Chaos.   Say, doth the dull soil
Quarrel with the proud forests it hath fed,
And feedeth still, more comely than itself ?
Can it deny the chiefdom of green groves ?   220
Or shall the tree be envious of the dove
Because it cooeth, and hath snowy wings
To wander wherewithal and find its joys ?
We are such forest-trees, and our fair boughs
Have bred forth, not pale solitary doves,   225
But eagles golden-feather'd, who do tower
Above us in their beauty, and must reign
In right thereof ; for 'tis the eternal law
That first in beauty should be first in might :
Yea, by that law, another race may drive   230
Our conquerors to mourn as we do now.
Have ye beheld the young God of the Seas,
My dispossessor ?   Have ye seen his face ?
Have ye beheld his chariot, foam'd along
By noble winged creatures he hath made ?   235
I saw him on the calmed waters scud,

With such a glow of beauty in his eyes,
That it enforc'd me to bid sad farewell
To all my empire : farewell sad I took,
And hither came, to see how dolorous fate   240
Had wrought upon ye ; and how I might best
Give consolation in this woe extreme.
Receive the truth, and let it be your balm."

   Whether through poz'd conviction, or disdain,
They guarded silence, when Oceanus   245
Left murmuring, what deepest thought can tell ?
But so it was, none answer'd for a space,
Save one whom none regarded, Clymene ;
And yet she answer'd not, only complain'd,
With hectic lips, and eyes up-looking mild,   250
Thus wording timidly among the fierce :
" O Father, I am here the simplest voice,
And all my knowledge is that joy is gone,
And this thing woe crept in among our hearts,
There to remain for ever, as I fear :   255
I would not bode of evil, if I thought
So weak a creature could turn off the help
Which by just right should come of mighty Gods ;
Yet let me tell my sorrow, let me tell
Of what I heard, and how it made me weep,   260
And know that we had parted from all hope.
I stood upon a shore, a pleasant shore,
Where a sweet clime was breathed from a land
Of fragrance, quietness, and trees, and flowers.
Full of calm joy it was, as I of grief ;   265
Too full of joy and soft delicious warmth ;
So that I felt a movement in my heart
To chide, and to reproach that solitude
With songs of misery, music of our woes ;
And sat me down, and took a mouthed shell   270

And murmur'd into it, and made melody
O melody no more ! for while I sang,
And with poor skill let pass into the breeze
The dull shell's echo, from a bowery strand
Just opposite, an island of the sea,   275
There came enchantment with the shifting wind,
That did both drown and keep alive my ears.
I threw my shell away upon the sand,
And a wave fill'd it, as my sense was fill'd
With that new blissful golden melody.   280
A living death was in each gush of sounds,
Each family of rapturous hurried notes,
That fell, one after one, yet all at once,
Like pearl beads dropping sudden from their string :
And then another, then another strain,   285
Each like a dove leaving its olive perch,
With music wing'd instead of silent plumes,
To hover round my head, and make me sick
Of joy and grief at once. Grief overcame,
And I was stopping up my frantic ears,   290
When, past all hindrance of my trembling hands,
A voice came sweeter, sweeter than all tune,
And still it cry'd, ' Apollo ! young Apollo !
' The morning-bright Apollo ! young Apollo ! '
I fled, it follow'd me, and cry'd ' Apollo ! '   295
O Father, and O Brethren, had ye felt
Those pains of mine ; O Saturn, hadst thou felt,
Ye would not call this too indulged tongue
Presumptuous, in thus venturing to be heard.''

So far her voice flow'd on, like timorous brook 300
That, lingering along a pebbled coast,
Doth fear to meet the sea : but sea it met,
And shudder'd ; for the overwhelming voice
Of huge Enceladus swallow'd it in wrath :

The ponderous syllables, like sullen waves 305
In the half-glutted hollows of reef-rocks,
Came booming thus, while still upon his arm
He lean'd ; not rising, from supreme contempt.
" Or shall we listen to the over-wise,
Or to the over-foolish giant, Gods ? 310
Not thunderbolt on thunderbolt, till all
That rebel Jove's whole armoury were spent,
Not world on world upon these shoulders piled,
Could agonize me more than baby-words
In midst of this dethronement horrible. 315
Speak ! roar ! shout ! yell ! ye sleepy Titans all.
Do ye forget the blows, the buffets vile ?
Are ye not smitten by a youngling arm ?
Dost thou forget, sham Monarch of the Waves,
Thy scalding in the seas ? What, have I rous'd 320
Your spleens with so few simple words as these ?
O joy ! for now I see ye are not lost :
O joy ! for now I see a thousand eyes
Wide glaring for revenge ! "—As this he said,
He lifted up his stature vast, and stood, 325
Still without intermission speaking thus :
" Now ye are flames, I'll tell you how to burn,
And purge the ether of our enemies ;
How to feed fierce the crooked stings of fire,
And singe away the swollen clouds of Jove, 330
Stifling that puny essence in its tent.
O let him feel the evil he hath done ;
For though I scorn Oceanus's lore,
Much pain have I for more than loss of realms :
The days of peace and slumberous calm are fled ; 335
Those days, all innocent of scathing war,
When all the fair Existences of heaven
Came open-eyed to guess what we would speak :—
That was before our brows were taught to frown,

Before our lips knew else but solemn sounds ;   340
That was before we knew the winged thing,
Victory, might be lost, or might be won.
And be ye mindful that Hyperion,
Our brightest brother, still is undisgraced—
Hyperion, lo ! his radiance is here ! "   345

   All eyes were on Enceladus's face,
And they beheld, while still Hyperion's name
Flew from his lips up to the vaulted rocks,
A pallid gleam across his features stern :
Not savage, for he saw full many a God   350
Wroth as himself.   He look'd upon them all,
And in each face he saw a gleam of light,
But splendider in Saturn's, whose hoar locks
Shone like the bubbling foam about a keel
When the prow sweeps into a midnight cove.   355
In pale and silver silence they remain'd,
Till suddenly a splendour, like the morn,
Pervaded all the beetling gloomy steeps,
All the sad spaces of oblivion,
And every gulf, and every chasm old,   360
And every height, and every sullen depth,
Voiceless, or hoarse with loud tormented streams :
And all the everlasting cataracts,
And all the headlong torrents far and near,
Mantled before in darkness and huge shade,   365
Now saw the light and made it terrible.
It was Hyperion :—a granite peak
His bright feet touch'd, and there he stay'd to view
The misery his brilliance had betray'd
To the most hateful seeing of itself.   370
Golden his hair of short Numidian curl,
Regal his shape majestic, a vast shade
In midst of his own brightness, like the bulk

Of Memnon's image at the set of sun
To one who travels from the dusking East :   375
Sighs, too, as mournful as that Memnon's harp
He utter'd, while his hands contemplative
He press'd together, and in silence stood.
Despondence seiz'd again the fallen Gods
At sight of the dejected King of Day,   380
And many hid their faces from the light :
But fierce Enceladus sent forth his eyes
Among the brotherhood ; and, at their glare,
Uprose Iapetus, and Creüs too,
And Phorcus, sea-born, and together strode   385
To where he towered on his eminence.
There those four shouted forth old Saturn's name ;
Hyperion from the peak loud answered, " Saturn ! "
Saturn sat near the Mother of the Gods,
In whose face was no joy, though all the Gods   390
Gave from their hollow throats the name of " Saturn ! "

BOOK III.

Thus in alternate uproar and sad peace,
Amazed were those Titans utterly.
O leave them, Muse ! O leave them to their woes ;
For thou art weak to sing such tumults dire :
A solitary sorrow best befits   5
Thy lips, and antheming a lonely grief.
Leave them, O Muse ! for thou anon wilt find
Many a fallen old Divinity
Wandering in vain about bewildered shores.
Meantime touch piously the Delphic harp,   10
And not a wind of heaven but will breathe
In aid soft warble from the Dorian flute ;
For lo ! 'tis for the Father of all verse.
Flush every thing that hath a vermeil hue,
Let the rose glow intense and warm the air,   15
And let the clouds of even and of morn
Float in voluptuous fleeces o'er the hills ;
Let the red wine within the goblet boil,
Cold as a bubbling well ; let faint-lipp'd shells,
On sands, or in great deeps, vermilion turn   20
Through all their labyrinths ; and let the maid
Blush keenly, as with some warm kiss surpris'd.
Chief isle of the embowered Cyclades,
Rejoice, O Delos, with thine olives green,
And poplars, and lawn-shading palms, and beech,   25
In which the Zephyr breathes the loudest song,

And hazels thick, dark-stemm'd beneath the shade :
Apollo is once more the golden theme !
Where was he, when the Giant of the Sun
Stood bright, amid the sorrow of his peers ?   30
Together had he left his mother fair
And his twin-sister sleeping in their bower,
And in the morning twilight wandered forth
Beside the osiers of a rivulet,
Full ankle-deep in lillies of the vale.   35
The nightingale had ceas'd, and a few stars
Were lingering in the heavens, while the thrush
Began calm-throated.   Throughout all the isle
There was no covert, no retired cave
Unhaunted by the murmurous noise of waves,   40
Though scarcely heard in many a green recess.
He listen'd, and he wept, and his bright tears
Went trickling down the golden bow he held.
Thus with half-shut suffused eyes he stood,
While from beneath some cumbrous boughs hard by 45
With solemn step an awful Goddess came,
And there was purport in her looks for him,
Which he with eager guess began to read
Perplex'd, the while melodiously he said :
" How cam'st thou over the unfooted sea ?   50
Or hath that antique mien and robed form
Mov'd in these vales invisible till now ?
Sure I have heard those vestments sweeping o'er
The fallen leaves, when I have sat alone
In cool mid-forest.   Surely I have traced   55
The rustle of those ample skirts about
These grassy solitudes, and seen the flowers
Lift up their heads, as still the whisper pass'd.
Goddess !   I have beheld those eyes before,
And their eternal calm, and all that face,   60
Or have I dream'd."—"Yes," said the supreme shape,

Thou hast dream'd of me ; and awaking up
Didst find a lyre all golden by thy side,
Whose strings touch'd by thy fingers, all the vast
Unwearied ear of the whole universe   65
Listen'd in pain and pleasure at the birth
Of such new tuneful wonder.   Is't not strange
That thou shouldst weep, so gifted ? Tell me, youth,
What sorrow thou canst feel ; for I am sad
When thou dost shed a tear : explain thy griefs   70
To one who in this lonely isle hath been
The watcher of thy sleep and hours of life,
From the young day when first thy infant hand
Pluck'd witless the weak flowers, till thine arm
Could bend that bow heroic to all times.   75
Show thy heart's secret to an ancient Power
Who hath forsaken old and sacred thrones
For prophecies of thee, and for the sake
Of loveliness new born."—Apollo then,
With sudden scrutiny and gloomless eyes,   80
Thus answer'd, while his white melodious throat
Throbb'd with the syllables.—" Mnemosyne !
Thy name is on my tongue, I know not how ;
Why should I tell thee what thou so well seest ?
Why should I strive to show what from thy lips   85
Would come no mystery ? For me, dark, dark,
And painful vile oblivion seals my eyes :
I strive to search wherefore I am so sad,
Until a melancholy numbs my limbs ;
And then upon the grass I sit, and moan,   90
Like one who once had wings.—O why should I
Feel curs'd and thwarted, when the liegeless air
Yields to my step aspirant ? why should I
Spurn the green turf as hateful to my feet ?
Goddess benign, point forth some unknown thing : 95
Are there not other regions than this isle ?

What are the stars ? There is the sun, the sun !
And the most patient brilliance of the moon !
And stars by thousands ! Point me out the way
To any one particular beauteous star,   100
And I will flit into it with my lyre,
And make its silvery splendour pant with bliss.
I have heard the cloudy thunder : Where is power ?
Whose hand, whose essence, what divinity
Makes this alarum in the elements,   105
While I here idle listen on the shores
In fearless yet in aching ignorance ?
O tell me, lonely Goddess, by thy harp,
That waileth every morn and eventide,
Tell me why thus I rave, about these groves !   110
Mute thou remainest—Mute ! yet I can read
A wondrous lesson in thy silent face :
Knowledge enormous makes a God of me.
Names, deeds, grey legends, dire events, rebellions,
Majesties, sovran voices, agonies,   115
Creations and destroyings, all at once
Pour into the wide hollows of my brain,
And deify me, as if some blithe wine
Or bright elixir peerless I had drunk,
And so become immortal."—Thus the God,   120
While his enkindled eyes, with level glance
Beneath his white soft temples, stedfast kept
Trembling with light upon Mnemosyne.
Soon wild commotions shook him, and made flush
All the immortal fairness of his limbs ;   125
Most like the struggle at the gate of death ;
Or liker still to one who should take leave
Of pale immortal death, and with a pang
As hot as death's is chill, with fierce convulse
Die into life : so young Apollo anguish'd :   130
His very hair, his golden tresses famed

Kept undulation round his eager neck.
During the pain Mnemosyne upheld
Her arms as one who prophesied.—At length
Apollo shriek'd ;—and lo ! from all his limbs   135
Celestial   *   *   *   *   *
*   *   *   *   *   *   *

NOTES.

HYPERION.

Hyperion was originally meant to be an epic in twelve books, but there is evidence that Keats abandoned this intention some time before he abandoned the poem, and that the poem, had he finished it, would not have exceeded four books. In this case Keats would not have attempted to narrate in detail the war of Enceladus and the giants against the Olympians, and the rest of the poem would have merely told us how Apollo went forth to fight Hyperion and how Hyperion, overcome by the beauty ·of his successor, found resistance impossible.

The poem opens with the despair of Saturn, chief of the second dynasty of gods, who with his fellow-gods has just been dethroned by his sons and daughters, the Olympians, as he and his dynasty in his youth, had himself dethroned his father Uranus and his fellows. He is roused by Thea, wife of Hyperion, the sun-god, who alone among his dynasty has not yet fallen. She leads him away to their friends. Meanwhile Hyperion descends to his palace, is shaken by evil omens, comforted by his father Coelus, who bears no resentment for his own earlier dethronement, and descends to earth. In Book II. Hyperion comes to the spot where the remnant of the conquered host, including Saturn and Thea, are gathered. Saturn calls for counsel. The sea-god advises acquiescence in their fate, since "'tis the eternal law that first in beauty should be first in might." Clymene tells how she heard the beauteous music of Apollo and Enceladus urges them to revenge. Hyperion then arrives.

Book III. tells how meanwhile Apollo, destined successor to Hyperion, is wandering in an isle when Mnemosyne visits him and dowers him with full divinity. Here the fragment ends.

The poem can thus be seen to have an allegorical significance—the greater beauty must always succeed the less, but, as we see both from the sufferings of the old gods and from the convulsive shrieks of Apollo the poet-god himself, only at the cost of pain;

29

the poet must feel the agony of the world before he gains full maturity.

Keats abandoned the poem because he felt that it was too Miltonic, that he was in danger of writing what was to him an alien tongue—an artificial dialect full of Latinisms and tricks of style. Certainly the wonderful way in which he has caught the very accent of Milton—mingled as it is with his own more human "romantic" notes—justifies his fears ; there was clearly a danger that he might leave the path natural to his genius. Moreover the fragment as we have it already parallels in many respects the early books of *Paradise Lost*, and, had the poem proceeded, it could hardly have failed to echo other situations treated by Milton, since the two themes have so much in common. Sublime as the fragment is, Keats's decision was therefore probably wise.

A few of the Miltonic echoes of the poem are pointed out in the notes, but in idea, in rhythm, in vocabulary, in the use of repetition, of inversion, of Latinisms, the debt is enormous : its extent can be realised only by reading Milton's great epic.

What Keats added was a power of pictorial representation, a human warmth, a sensuous love of the beauties of Nature not characteristic of Milton—note especially the splendour of Hyperion's palace and his entry to it, and the sublime description of the dejected Saturn which recalls some vast statue of the early world.

BOOK I.

1. shady sadness : "gloomy shade "; this use of abstractions is frequent in Keats : here it serves to give the gloom instead of the shade first importance.

3. eve's one star : Venus, the evening star, which appears long before the others : the slow movement of the three heavy stresses suggests the peace of evening.

4. Saturn : the chief of the ancient dynasty of gods, father of Jupiter, Neptune, etc., and identified by the Romans with the Greek Cronos. He was the youngest of the Titans, son of Uranus and Ge (Heaven and Earth) and dethroned his father Uranus. The striking simile is reminiscent of Chaucer's "domb as any stoon " (*Hous of Fame*, II. 656).

6. hung about his head : *i.e.* "rose above him, on the sides of the valley."

10. But where . . . rest : one of Keats's perfect little pictures, showing the close observation of the Nature-lover.

11-14. still . . . lips : the Naiad, or nymph of the stream, has hushed the ripples to silence, awed by the shade of the fallen god.

18 nerveless : "without strength "; the succession of epithets and the pause after *unsceptred* give an effect of heavy despair.

19. **realmless** : " no longer possessing a kingdom " ; the adjective is transferred from Saturn to his eyes.

20-1. **Earth . . . mother** : see note on line 4.

27-8 **By her . . . height** : "compared with her one of the Amazons, the mythical warrior-women of Asia Minor, would have seemed no taller than a pigmy." **Had** : subjunctive, *would have.*

29. **Achilles** : the mighty hero of Homer's *Iliad* ; he led the Greeks against Troy.

30. **Ixion** : for ungrateful treachery to Zeus, Ixion king of the Lapithae was chained by the hands and feet to a perpetually revolving wheel.

31. **Memphian sphinx** : a sphinx or stone monster, part lion, part woman, at Memphis, formerly the second greatest city of Egypt, about 10 miles above the Pyramids.

33. **when . . . lore** : " when Egypt was the centre of learning " ; cp. Acts vii. 22.

35-6. **How . . . self** : *i.e.* " her face would have been called beautiful, if the expression of sorrow upon it had not been more beautiful than its form " ; such fantastic ideas are called conceits.

37. **there was . . . in her regard** : a splendid example of Keats's concise and vivid phrasing " she looked as if she were listening and afraid."

39-41. **As if the vanward . . . up** : " as if the storm of misfortune had just begun, the first clouds having burst only to be followed by the thunder of the full tempest." Within the metaphor of the storm there is a second metaphor of battle ; it is such compressed imagery which gives Keats's style its richness and dignity.

48. **In solemn tenour** : " of solemn purport."

50-1. **O how . . . Gods !** : " how feeble (is our language) compared to the mighty speech of the early gods."

61. **reluctant** : besides the modern meaning, there is here a hint of the original (and Miltonic) significance, " struggling violently."

65-7. **All . . . breathe** : " as each moment passes, it makes the wretched truth more evident and forces it upon our grief-stricken minds so that it is impossible for us to disbelieve it."

74. **branch-charmed** : " with their branches charmed into stillness." **earnest** : another of Keats's exquisite epithets.

83-4 **One . . . night** : " one moon had slowly changed from new through her four quarters to full," *i.e.* a month had passed.

86. **natural . . . cavern** : Keats is probably thinking of Fingal's Cave in the Isle of Staffa, which he elsewhere called a " cathedral of the sea."

87. **frozen** : *i.e.* motionless through grief. **couchant** : lying.

90-4. Such a succession of simple sentences joined by *and* is characteristic of epic style—the construction gives simplicity, continuity, and dignity.

94. **horrid** : " standing on end "—the original meaning of the word (Latin *horreo*), which later came to mean " causing the hair to stand on end with fright." **aspen-malady** : one of Keats's pregnant compound words, meaning " sickness which made him tremble like an aspen tree."

96. **Thea** : Thia, sister of Saturn and wife of Hyperion, to whom she bore Helios (the sun), Eos (Aurora), and Selene (the moon). Hyperion was thus really the father of the sun, not the sun himself.

105. **nervous** : " strong, vigorous."

108. **influence benign . . . pale** : " kindly rule of the (movements of the) white planets " : the placing of the adjectives after the noun is a Miltonic device.

112-16. **I am gone . . . earth** : " I am no longer myself, since I have lost my power ; when I fell from my throne in Heaven all that made me what I was left me."

117. **eterne** : " eternal." **sphere** : " roll."

118 **lorn of light** : " unlighted " ; *lorn* was originally the past participle of *lose* ; hence *bereft*.

119. **region'd with life-air** : " made a region filled with air, which alone makes life possible." **barren void** : " space empty of air and so unable to produce life."

120. **yawn** : " gulf."

125. **be of ripe progress** : " go on satisfactorily."

129. **metropolitan** : " of the chief city " (of the gods).

130. **voices of soft proclaim** : " voices which make proclamation in gentle accents." **silver . . . shells** : " the silvery notes of instruments made by stretching across hollow shells."

136. **Druid** : the Druids or ancient British priests are generally represented as old men with long, white hair.

138. **fever out** : " start out from his head, bright with fever."

140. **snatch'd utterance** : " spoke," but the phrase admirably suggests sudden desperate speech.

145. **chaos** : " the primeval confusion from which the universe was formed." Saturn asks where he can find raw material for another universe.

146. **Olympus** : the mountain of Thessaly in Greece upon which the gods were supposed to live.

147. **rebel three** : *i.e.* Jupiter, Neptune, and Pluto, who had usurped rule over heaven, the sea, and Hades respectively.

156-7. **like . . . nest** : as often with Keats, the simile has also a secondary appropriateness—if the boughs yield like mist, Saturn and Thea are " upmounting " like eagles, the royal birds.

161. **Titans** : *i.e.* the other Titans. The Titans were the six sons and daughters of Uranus and Ge, who, after their parents were dethroned, formed a dynasty of gods, Saturn being chief among them. They were in turn dethroned by the sons of Saturn, headed by Zeus (Jupiter). **self-hid** : " having hidden themselves." **prison-bound** : " fettered and imprisoned."

162. **groan'd . . . allegiance** : " groaned with longing for the rule of their old leader Saturn."

164. **mammoth-brood** : " mighty race " of Titans.

166. **on his orbed fire** : " on the blazing globe of the sun."

171. **dog's . . . screech** : the howling of dogs and the screeching of owls were supposed to foretell disaster.

172-3. **familiar . . . bell** : " the appearance of the ghost of a friend at the first note of a bell tolled for his death."

174. **prophesying . . . lamp** : omens were read into the way in which a wick burnt down, etc.

175. **portion'd** : " proportioned," *i.e.* the horrors were as much greater than ordinary horrors as Hyperion's nerves were stronger than human nerves.

177. **bastion'd** : *i.e.* protected by bastions or fortifications projecting from the angles of a rampart.

181. **Aurorian** : belonging to Aurora, the goddess of the dawn.

182. **angerly** : a more striking word than *angrily* : Keats probably took it from Shakespeare's *King John,* IV. i. 82.

183-5. These almost identical lines give the haunting beauty peculiar to refrains, besides emphasising the strangeness of the omens.

188. **metal sick** : a reference to the unpleasant taste of metals.

192. **For** : " instead of."

197. **minions** : " followers, retainers."

204. **slope** : " moving on a slope " ; this use of the word is Miltonic.

206. **solemn tubes** : *i.e.* trumpets.

207. **Zephyrs** : " breezes " . Zephyrus was the west wind.

209. **vermeil** : vermilion, rosy.

211. **inlet** : " entrance," another Miltonic word.

216. **Hours** : the daughters of Zeus (Jupiter) : their dove-wings seem to be Keats's invention, since they are generally represented as wingless.

226. **despite of godlike curb** : " in spite of his divine attempt to repress his feelings."

227. **dreams** : *i.e.* the portentous shapes, " horrors portion'd to a giant nerve," which had appeared to foretell his ruin, the lank-ear'd Phantoms of line 230.

246. **Tellus and her briny robes** : *i.e.* the earth and the sea which surrounds it.

249. **ınfant thunderer, rebel Jove** : Jove (Jupiter) or Zeus had driven his father from the throne by hurlıng thunderbolts.

253-5. **For . . . Hush !** : perhaps the only passage in the poem which, under the ınfluence of the " Cockney school," falls below epıc dıgnity.

262. **convuls'd** : *i.e.* rolled back convulsively : there is here some-thıng of the force of the Latın *convulsum* ; the word is one of Keats's favourites.

274. **broad-belting colure** : the *colures* are the two cırcles of the celestıal sphere, supposed to ıntersect each other ın points corre-spondıng to the terrestrial poles. Keats probably took the word from Mılton.

276. **nadir** : the part of the heavens dırectly under our feet, the lowest poınt, opposite the *zenıth* or hıghest poınt.

287. **outspreaded** : probably Keats thought thıs a more graphic and dıgnıfied form than *outspread.*

288. **dazzling . . . eclipse** : *ı.e.* the globe remained dark untıl Hyperıon commanded lıght to appear, that is, untıl the sun rose.

296. **sisterly** : " lıke two sisters."

297. **sail** : " make to sail."

298. **dusk demesnes** : " dark domınıons."

307. **Coelus** : the Latin equivalent of Uranus (see lınes 309-10, and note on lıne 4) ; Keats, in opposıtion to the legendary account, makes hım pity hıs dethroned offspring instead of rejoıcıng revenge-fully that they have met the doom which he suffered at their hands.

311-12. **All unrevealed . . . creating** : unknown even to thy parents.

315. **at . . . thereof** : *i.e.* at hıs children, the chıldren of earth and sky.

319-20. **Of these . . . goddesses** : *i.e.* " thou, thy brethren and the goddesses are among these new-form'd manıfestatıons."

326. **wox** : " grew."

338. **an evıdent god** : " obvıously divine, not dethroned and powerless as I am."

340. **ethereal** : " heavenly."

343-5. **Be . . . circumstance** : " do thou therefore lead events instead of awaitıng them." **seize . . . murmur** : " seize the point of the arrow aımed at thee before the taut bowstrıng hums as the arrow is shot," *i.e.* anticipate attack.

349. **region-whisper** : " whisper from the heavenly regions."

354. **inclıne** : " ınclination, bendıng."

BOOK II.

1-4. **Just . . . mourn'd** · these lines link the close of Book I. to the events immediately following those narrated in Book I., lines 155-7.

4. **Cybele :** or Rhea, a daughter of Uranus and the wife of Saturn.

5. **insulting :** the word keeps something of the original force of *leaping in* and something of the derived sense of jumping upon a fallen foe.

7. **for :** " in consequence of."

9. **Pouring . . . where :** " constantly pouring down the same volume of water, without any knowledge of the direction taken " : the extreme compression is again characteristic of the Miltonic style.

17. **stubborn'd :** " made stubborn or firm."

19. **Coeus . . . Briarëus :** sons of Uranus and Ge ; Gyges and Briareus were giants with 100 arms and 50 heads. Here Keats, like Milton, uses a succession of proper names to add sonority to the verse.

20. **Typhon :** a monster, described sometimes as a hurricane (hence *typhoon*) and sometimes as a fire-breathing giant.

Dolor : there was no Titan or giant of this name, but Keats apparently took the name from the Latin author Hyginus, where the personified abstraction *Dolor* (grief) is mentioned in close connection with the Titans. **Porphyrion :** one of the giants who fought on the side of Saturn against Jupiter.

22. **pent . . . breath :** " confined in places where it was hard to breathe."

23. **opaque element :** " thick air."

28. **sanguine . . . pulse :** " with fevered, pulsing flow of blood."

29. **Mnemosyne :** Memory, a daughter of Uranus.

30 **Phoebe :** daughter of Uranus and Ge, and really the grand-mother of the moon-goddess Phoebe. Keats here confuses the two goddesses.

32. **for the main :** " for the most part." **covert** · " shelter."

33. **scarce . . . life :** " scarcely appearing to live."

34. **cirque . . . moor :** Keats obviously has Stonehenge in mind : the pictorial simile is one of his finest.

41. **Creüs :** another son of Uranus and brother of Saturn, as were also Iapetus (l. 44), and Cottus (l. 49) who was not a Titan but a giant like Briareus (see note on Book II., l. 19).

45. **plashy :** " speckled, as if with splashes of dye."

46. **gorge :** " throat."

47. **and because :** *i e.* " and it was dead because."

53. **Asia :** generally reputed the daughter of Oceanus and Tethys. Keats gives her a new parentage—Tellus, the Earth, and Kaf, a

mythical mountain mentioned in the Arabian Nights. She is identified with the continent Asia ; hence *dusky face* (l. 56).

55. **though feminine** : it would be interesting to know what incident, when he walked the hospitals, gave Keats the curious idea that it is easier to bear girls than boys.

61. **as hope . . . leans** : critics have objected to this mingling of classical mythology and hope with her anchor, but all the great Elizabethan writers draw indiscriminately upon pagan and Christian symbolism.

66. **shadow'd Enceladus** : *i.e.* Enceladus cast a shadow ; Enceladus was usually identified with Typhon, but Keats makes them two persons.

70. **was hurling** : *i.e.* imagined himself already hurling. **second war** : *i.e.* the war against Zeus, in which the Titans hurled mountains at him.

73. **Atlas** : son of Iapetus and Asia : he later took part in the Titans' war against Zeus and was condemned as a punishment to bear heaven on his head and hands.

74. **Phorcus . . . Gorgons** : Phorcus was a sea-god, the son of Pontus and Ge ; Ceto bore him the three monstrous maidens, the gorgons, whose hair was serpents and who had wings, brazen claws and enormous teeth. Medusa, who alone of the gorgons was mortal, was killed by Perseus : her head was so terrible that anyone looking upon it was changed into stone.

75 **Oceanus** : he was the one Titan who had not joined in war against Zeus and the other Olympians.

76. **Clymene** : generally identified with Asia, whom, however, Keats made a different goddess with different parents (see note on Book II., l. 53).

77. **Themis** : another daughter of Uranus and Ge.

78. **Ops** : identical with Cybele (see note on Book II., l. 4).

79 **more than** : we should say *any more than.*

82. **when the Muse's . . . flight ?** : *i.e.* " when the poet is about to sing a loftier strain, who shall delay him ? " The nine Muses, daughters of Zeus and Mnemosyne, were the goddesses who inspired song ; later, they were regarded as presiding over the different kinds of poetry and the arts and sciences.

92. **supreme** : the word is here probably stressed on both syllables, thus emphasising the majesty of Saturn.

95. **spleen** : " anger," the spleen being formerly considered the seat of anger.

97. **mortal** : probably *such that it changed him to a mortal,* i.e. robbed him of his divinity ; actually, of course, Saturn, though dethroned, did not lose his immortality.

98. disanointing : *i e.* such that it undid the effects of the anointing oil used at a coronation : Saturn is no longer king.

99. kept her still : " kept herself motionless."

120. utterless : " unutterable."

122. Such . . . pines : the echo-effect of this half-repetition of l. 116 itself suggests the reverberant roar in the pines.

128. dinn'd : " filled with noise ", for the conciseness attained by the coinage, cp. *mountain'd world* in l. 123. silverly : *silver,* as applied to sound, is one of Keats's favourite words.

133. spirit-leaved book : presumably *book whose leaves were written by spirits* : the book appears to be Keats's invention.

140. element : there were thought to be four elements—earth, air, fire, and water—out of which everything else was composed.

153. the first-born . . . gods : Saturn and his brothers and sisters were the first gods to be born : Uranus sprang from primeval Chaos. See below, ll. 191-200.

155. untremendous : " not to be trembled at."

165. astonied : " astonished."

168. Sophist . . . grove : the sophists of ancient Athens were wise men (sages) who taught, often out-of-doors, philosophy, rhetoric, and politics.

171. first-endeavouring : a reference to the fact that he is *beginning* his speech.

176. bellows unto ire : " incitement to anger," anger being treated as a fire.

183. atom-universe : a reference to the theory developed by Lucretius (95 B.C.–52 B.C.) in his *De Rerum Natura* that the whole universe is formed from minute atoms.

185. only . . . supremacy . *i.e.* Saturn is so high above others that he misses small points obvious to meaner minds.

192. Light . . . broil : *i.e.* light, which sprang from the internal conflict of darkness and chaos.

202. to whom 'tis pain : " pain, that is, for those who find truth painful."

204-5 to envisage . . . sovereignty : " the true height of supremacy is the ability to look facts in the face calmly."

208 show beyond : " appear superior to."

214 pass : " surpass." 240. dolorous : " sad."

244. poz'd : " posed, perplexed, at a loss for a retort."

250. hectic : " fevered."

256. bode of evil : " prophesy evil."

270. mouthed shell : some of the earliest musical instruments were made from the shells of animals.

277. drown . . . ears : " deafen me and make me listen.''

293. Apollo : the god of poetry and song, son of Zeus.

304. Enceladus : see note on Book II., l. 66.

305 the ponderous waves : the whole of this passage gives one of the best examples of Keats's use of onomatopoeia and word-harmony.

310. Or to . . . Gods : it has been ingeniously conjectured that the true reading should be *Or to the over-foolish, giant-gods* ?

312. Jove : Zeus, son of Saturn, who had led the rebellion, showering thunderbolts upon his father and the other ancient gods.

319-20. Dost . . . seas : Enceladus is addressing Oceanus, who was cast down into the sea by the revolting Olympian deities.

365 mantled : " covered as with a mantle."

369-70. the misery . . . itself : *i.e.* the wretchedness of the dethroned gods, who could now, in the light of Hyperion the sun-god, see how miserable they appeared.

371. Numidian : Numidia was the name of a country of N. Africa ; the reference is thus to the short curly hair of the negroes.

374. Memnon's image : there was a statue of Memnon, the son of Tithonus and Aurora (the dawn), near Thebes, which uttered a mournful sound when the first beams of the sun struck it, as if Memnon were greeting his mother.

BOOK III.

5-6. A solitary . . . grief : Keats's brother Tom had just died. antheming : " commemorating in an anthem."

9. bewildered : a transferred epithet , in sense it qualifies *Divinity*.

10. Delphic : connected with Delphi, a small town in Greece, famous for its oracle of Apollo, the god of poetry and of the sun.

12. Dorian : the Dorians, one of the great Greek tribes, whose name is associated with a special mode of music, characterised by its severe tone, and particularly suited for religious and martial occasions.

13. Father of all verse : Apollo.

23. Cyclades : a group of islands in the Aegean Sea, which lay in a circle round Delos, the most important of them : upon Delos Latona bore Apollo and his twin-sister Artemis.

26. In which . . . song : " in which there is no wind harsher than Zephyr, the West wind."

29. Giant of the Sun : Hyperion.

43. golden bow : Apollo is frequently represented in ancient art with a bow and arrows : his bow is here golden, probably because he is the sun-god who shoots golden rays.

44. **suffused** : " filled with tears."

46. **an awful goddess** : Mnemosyne or Memory, daughter of Uranus and mother of the Muses. See l. 82.

74. **witless** · " unconsciously " ; "without thought."

92. **liegeless** : " without a liege-lord, unconquered."

93. **aspirant** : " aspiring."

114. **grey** : " old," a notable example of Keats's instinctive choice of a beautiful epithet.

115. **sovran** : " sovereign."

119. **peerless** : " unequalled " ; the placing of the noun *elixir* between two adjectives is a Miltonic device.

128. **pale immortal death** : another of Keats's beautiful and pregnant phrases : see also the striking *die into life* (l. 130).

129. **convulse** : " convulsion."

132. **kept undulation** : " waved incessantly."

ISABELLA ;

OR

THE POT OF BASIL.

I.

FAIR Isabel, poor simple Isabel !
  Lorenzo, a young palmer in Love's eye !
They could not in the self-same mansion dwell
  Without some stir of heart, some malady ;
They could not sit at meals but feel how well   5
  It soothed each to be the other by ;
They could not, sure, beneath the same roof sleep
But to each other dream, and nightly weep.

II.

With every morn their love grew tenderer,
  With every eve deeper and tenderer still ;   10
He might not in house, field, or garden stir,
  But her full shape would all his seeing fill ;
And his continual voice was pleasanter
  To her, than noise of trees or hidden rill ;
Her lute-string gave an echo of his name,   15
She spoilt her half-done broidery with the same.

III.

He knew whose gentle hand was at the latch
  Before the door had given her to his eyes ;
And from her chamber-window he would catch
  Her beauty farther than the falcon spies ;   20

41

And constant as her vespers would he watch,
  Because her face was turn'd to the same skies ;
And with sick longing all the night outwear,
To hear her morning-step upon the stair.

IV.

A whole long month of May in this sad plight   25
  Made their cheeks paler by the break of June :
" To-morrow will I bow to my delight,
  To-morrow will I ask my lady's boon."—
" O may I never see another night,
  Lorenzo, if thy lips breathe not love's tune."—   30
So spake they to their pillows ; but, alas,
Honeyless days and days did he let pass ;

V.

Until sweet Isabella's untouch'd cheek
  Fell sick within the rose's just domain,
Fell thin as a young mother's, who doth seek   35
  By every lull to cool her infant's pain :
" How ill she is," said he, " I may not speak,
  And yet I will, and tell my love all plain :
If looks speak love-laws, I will drink her tears,
And at the least 'twill startle off her cares."   40

VI.

So said he one fair morning, and all day
  His heart beat awfully against his side ;
And to his heart he inwardly did pray
  For power to speak ; but still the ruddy tide
Stifled his voice, and puls'd resolve away—   45
  Fever'd his high conceit of such a bride,
Yet brought him to the meekness of a child :
Alas ! when passion is both meek and wild !

VII.

So once more he had wak'd and anguished
  A dreary night of love and misery,   50
If Isabel's quick eye had not been wed
  To every symbol on his forehead high ;
She saw it waxing very pale and dead,
  And straight all flush'd ; so, lisped tenderly,
" Lorenzo ! "—here she ceas'd her timid quest,   55
But in her tone and look he read the rest.

VIII.

" O Isabella, I can half perceive
  That I may speak my grief into thine ear ;
If thou didst ever anything believe,
  Believe how I love thee, believe how near   60
My soul is to its doom : I would not grieve
  Thy hand by unwelcome pressing, would not fear
Thine eyes by gazing ; but I cannot live
Another night, and not my passion shrive.

IX.

" Love ! thou art leading me from wintry cold,   65
  Lady ! thou leadest me to summer clime,
And I must taste the blossoms that unfold
  In its ripe warmth this gracious morning time."
So said, his erewhile timid lips grew bold,
  And poesied with hers in dewy rhyme :   70
Great bliss was with them, and great happiness
Grew, like a lusty flower in June's caress.

X.

Parting they seem'd to tread upon the air,
  Twin roses by the zephyr blown apart

Only to meet again more close, and share   75
   The inward fragrance of each other's heart.
She, to her chamber gone, a ditty fair
   Sang, of delicious love and honey'd dart ;
He with light steps went up a western hill,
And bade the sun farewell, and joy'd his fill.   80

XI.

All close they met again, before the dusk
   Had taken from the stars its pleasant veil,
All close they met, all eves, before the dusk
   Had taken from the stars its pleasant veil,
Close in a bower of hyacinth and musk,   85
   Unknown of any, free from whispering tale.
Ah ! better had it been for ever so,
Than idle ears should pleasure in their woe.

XII.

Were they unhappy then ?—It cannot be—
   Too many tears for lovers have they shed,   90
Too many sighs give we to them in fee,
   Too much of pity after they are dead,
Too many doleful stories do we see,
   Whose matter in bright gold were best be read ;
Except in such a page where Theseus' spouse   95
Over the pathless waves towards him bows.

XIII.

But, for the general award of love,
   The little sweet doth kill much bitterness ;
Though Dido silent is in under-grove,
   And Isabella's was a great distress,   100
Though young Lorenzo in warm Indian clove
   Was not embalm'd, this truth is not the less—

Even bees, the little almsmen of spring-bowers,
Know there is richest juice in poison-flowers.

XIV.

With her two brothers this fair lady dwelt,   105
   Enriched from ancestral merchandize,
And for them many a weary hand did swelt
   In torched mines and noisy factories,
And many once proud quiver'd loins did melt
   In blood from stinging whip ;—with hollow eyes   110
Many all day in dazzling river stood,
To take the rich-or'd driftings of the flood.

XV.

For them the Ceylon diver held his breath,
   And went all naked to the hungry shark ;
For them his ears gush'd blood ; for them in death   115
   The seal on the cold ice with piteous bark
Lay full of darts ; for them alone did seethe
   A thousand men in troubles wide and dark :
Half-ignorant, they turn'd an easy wheel,
That set sharp racks at work, to pinch and peel.   120

XVI.

Why were they proud ?   Because their marble founts
   Gush'd with more pride than do a wretch's tears ?—
Why were they proud ?   Because fair orange-mounts
   Were of more soft ascent than lazar stairs ?—
Why were they proud ?   Because red-lin'd accounts   125
   Were richer than the songs of Grecian years ?—
Why were they proud ? again we ask aloud,
Why in the name of Glory were they proud ?

XVII.

Yet were these Florentines as self-retired
  In hungry pride and gainful cowardice,   130
As two close Hebrews in that land inspired,
  Pal'd in and vineyarded from beggar-spies ;
The hawks of ship-mast forests—the untired
  And pannier'd mules for ducats and old lies—
Quick cat's-paws on the generous stray-away,—   135
Great wits in Spanish, Tuscan, and Malay.

XVIII.

How was it these same ledger-men could spy
  Fair Isabella in her downy nest ?
How could they find out in Lorenzo's eye
  A straying from his toil ?   Hot Egypt's pest   140
Into their vision covetous and sly !
  How could these money-bags see east and west ?—
Yet so they did—and every dealer fair
Must see behind, as doth the hunted hare.

XIX.

O eloquent and famed Boccaccio !   145
  Of thee we now should ask forgiving boon,
And of thy spicy myrtles as they blow,
  And of thy roses amorous of the moon,
And of thy lilies, that do paler grow
  Now they can no more hear thy ghittern's tune, 150
For venturing syllables that ill beseem
The quiet glooms of such a piteous theme.

XX.

Grant thou a pardon here, and then the tale
  Shall move on soberly, as it is meet ;

There is no other crime, no mad assail 155
   To make old prose in modern rhyme more sweet :
But it is done—succeed the verse or fail—
   To honour thee, and thy gone spirit greet ;
To stead thee as a verse in English tongue,
An echo of thee in the north-wind sung. 160

XXI.

These brethren having found by many signs
   What love Lorenzo for their sister had,
And how she lov'd him too, each unconfines
   His bitter thoughts to other, well nigh mad
That he, the servant of their trade designs, 165
   Should in their sister's love be blithe and glad,
When 'twas their plan to coax her by degrees
To some high noble and his olive-trees.

XXII.

And many a jealous conference had they,
   And many times they bit their lips alone, 170
Before they fix'd upon a surest way
   To make the youngster for his crime atone ;
And at the last, these men of cruel clay
   Cut Mercy with a sharp knife to the bone ;
For they resolved in some forest dim 175
To kill Lorenzo, and there bury him.

XXIII.

So on a pleasant morning, as he leant
   Into the sun-rise, o'er the balulstrade
Of the garden-terrace, towards him they bent
   Their footing through the dews ; and to him said, 180
" You seem there in the quiet of content,
   Lorenzo, and we are most loth to invade

Calm speculation ; but if you are wise,
Bestride your steed while cold is in the skies.

XXIV.

To-day we purpose, aye, this hour we mount   185
   To spur three leagues towards the Apennine ;
Come down, we pray thee, ere the hot sun count
   His dewy rosary on the eglantine."
Lorenzo, courteously, as he was wont,
   Bow'd a fair greeting to these serpents' whine ;   190
And went in haste, to get in readiness,
With belt, and spur, and bracing huntsman's dress.

XXV.

And as he to the court-yard pass'd along,
   Each third step did he pause, and listen'd oft
If he could hear his lady's matin-song,   195
   Or the light whisper of her footstep soft ;
And as he thus over his passion hung,
   He heard a laugh full musical aloft ;
When, looking up, he saw her features bright
Smile through an in-door lattice, all delight.   200

XXVI.

" Love, Isabel ! " said he, " I was in pain
   Lest I should miss to bid thee a good morrow :
Ah ! what if I should lose thee, when so fain
   I am to stifle all the heavy sorrow
Of a poor three hours' absence ? but we'll gain   205
   Out of the amorous dark what day doth borrow.
Good bye ! I'll soon be back."—"Good bye ! " said she :—
And as he went she chanted merrily.

XXVII.

So the two brothers and their murder'd man
    Rode past fair Florence, to where Arno's stream   210
Gurgles through straiten'd banks, and still doth fan
    Itself with dancing bulrush, and the bream
Keeps head against the freshets. Sick and wan
    The brothers' faces in the ford did seem,
Lorenzo's flush with love.—They pass'd the water   215
Into a forest quiet for the slaughter.

XXVIII.

There was Lorenzo slain and buried in,
    There in that forest did his great love cease ;
Ah ! when a soul doth thus its freedom win,
    It aches in loneliness—is ill at peace   220
As the break-covert blood-hounds of such sin :
    They dipp'd their swords in the water, and did tease
Their horses homeward, with convulsed spur,
Each richer by his being a murderer.

XXIX.

They told their sister how, with sudden speed,   225
    Lorenzo had ta'en ship for foreign lands,
Because of some great urgency and need
    In their affairs, requiring trusty hands.
Poor girl ! put on thy stifling widow's weed,
    And 'scape at once from Hope's accursed bands ; 230
To-day thou wilt not see him, nor to-morrow,
And the next day will be a day of sorrow.

XXX.

She weeps alone for pleasures not to be ;
    Sorely she wept until the night came on,

KTS.   4

And then, in stead of love, O misery !   235
　　She brooded o'er the luxury alone :　·
His image in the dusk she seem'd to see,
　　And to the silence made a gentle moan,
Spreading her perfect arms upon the air,
And on her couch low murmuring " Where ? O where ? " 240

XXXI.

But Selfishness, Love's cousin, held not long
　　Its fiery vigil in her single breast ;
She fretted for the golden hour, and hung
　　Upon the time with feverish unrest—
Not long—for soon into her heart a throng   245
　　Of higher occupants, a richer zest,
Came tragic ; passion not to be subdu'd,
And sorrow for her love in travels rude.

XXXII.

In the mid days of autumn, on their eves
　　The breath of Winter comes from far away,   250
And the sick west continually bereaves
　　Of some gold tinge, and plays a roundelay
Of death among the bushes and the leaves,
　　To make all bare before he dares to stray
From his north cavern.　So sweet Isabel   255
By gradual decay from beauty fell,

XXXIII.

Because Lorenzo came not.　Oftentimes
　　She ask'd her brothers, with an eye all pale,
Striving to be itself, what dungeon climes
　　Could keep him off so long ?　They spake a tale   260
Time after time, to quiet her.　Their crimes
　　Came on them, like a smoke from Hinnom's vale ;

And every night in dreams they groan'd aloud,
To see their sister in her snowy shroud.

XXXIV.

And she had died in drowsy ignorance,   265
    But for a thing more deadly dark than all ;
It came like a fierce potion, drunk by chance,
    Which saves a sick man from the feather'd pall
For some few gasping moments ; like a lance,
    Waking an Indian from his cloudy hall   270
With cruel pierce, and bringing him again
Sense of the gnawing fire at heart and brain.

XXXV.

It was a vision.——In the drowsy gloom,
    The dull of midnight, at her couch's foot
Lorenzo stood, and wept : the forest tomb   275
    Had marr'd his glossy hair which once could shoot
Lustre into the sun, and put cold doom
    Upon his lips, and taken the soft lute
From his lorn voice, and past his loamed ears
Had made a miry channel for his tears.   280

XXXVI.

Strange sound it was, when the pale shadow spake ;
    For there was striving, in its piteous tongue,
To speak as when on earth it was awake,
    And Isabella on its music hung :
Languor there was in it, and tremulous shake,   285
    As in a palsied Druid's harp unstrung ;
And through it moan'd a ghostly under-song,
Like hoarse night-gusts sepulchral briars among.

XXXVII.

Its eyes, though wild, were still all dewy bright
   With love, and kept all phantom fear aloof   290
From the poor girl by magic of their light,
   The while it did unthread the horrid woof
Of the late darken'd time,—the murderous spite
   Of pride and avarice,—the dark pine roof
In the forest,—and the sodden turfed dell,   295
Where, without any word, from stabs he fell.

XXXVIII.

Saying moreover, " Isabel, my sweet !
   Red whortle-berries droop above my head,
And a large flint-stone weighs upon my feet ;
   Around me beeches and high chestnuts shed   300
Their leaves and prickly nuts ; a sheep-fold bleat
   Comes from beyond the river to my bed :
Go, shed one tear upon my heather-bloom,
And it shall comfort me within the tomb.

XXXIX.

I am a shadow now, alas ! alas !   305
   Upon the skirts of human-nature dwelling
Alone : I chant alone the holy mass,
   While little sounds of life are round me kneeling,
And glossy bees at noon do fieldward pass,
   And many a chapel bell the hour is telling,   310
Paining me through : those sounds grow strange to me,
And thou art distant in Humanity.

XL.

I know what was, I feel full well what is,
   And I should rage, if spirits could go mad ;

Though I forget the taste of earthly bliss,   315
   That paleness warms my grave, as though I had
A Seraph chosen from the bright abyss
   To be my spouse : thy paleness makes me glad ;
Thy beauty grows upon me, and I feel
A greater love through all my essence steal."   320

XLI.

The Spirit mourn'd " Adieu ! "—dissolv'd and left
   The atom darkness in a slow turmoil ;
As when of healthful midnight sleep bereft,
   Thinking on rugged hours and fruitless toil,
We put our eyes into a pillowy cleft,   325
   And see the spangly gloom froth up and boil :
It made sad Isabella's eyelids ache,
And in the dawn she started up awake ;

XLII.

" Ha ! ha ! " said she, " I knew not this hard life,
   I thought the worst was simple misery ;   330
I thought some Fate with pleasure or with strife
   Portion'd us—happy days, or else to die ;
But there is crime—a brother's bloody knife !
   Sweet Spirit, thou hast school'd my infancy :
I'll visit thee for this, and kiss thine eyes,   335
And greet thee morn and even in the skies."

XLIII.

When the full morning came, she had devised
   How she might secret to the forest hie ;
How she might find the clay, so dearly prized,
   And sing to it one latest lullaby ;   340
How her short absence might be unsurmised,
   While she the inmost of the dream would try.

Resolv'd, she took with her an aged nurse,
And went into that dismal forest-hearse.

XLIV.

See, as they creep along the river side,   345
   How she doth whisper to that aged Dame,
And, after looking round the champaign wide,
   Shows her a knife.—" What feverous hectic flame
Burns in thee, child ?—What good can thee betide,
   That thou should'st smile again ? "—The evening came,
And they had found Lorenzo's earthy bed ;   351
The flint was there, the berries at his head.

XLV.

Who hath not loiter'd in a green church-yard,
   And let his spirit, like a demon-mole,
Work through the clayey soil and gravel hard,   355
   To see scull, coffin'd bones, and funeral stole ;
Pitying each form that hungry Death hath marr'd,
   And filling it once more with human soul ?
Ah ! this is holiday to what was felt
When Isabella by Lorenzo knelt.   360

XLVI.

She gaz'd into the fresh-thrown mould, as though
   One glance did fully all its secrets tell ;
Clearly she saw, as other eyes would know
   Pale limbs at bottom of a crystal well ;
Upon the murderous spot she seem'd to grow,   365
   Like to a native lily of the dell :
Then with her knife, all sudden, she began
To dig more fervently than misers can.

XLVII.

Soon she turn'd up a soiled glove, whereon
   Her silk had play'd in purple phantasies,   370
She kiss'd it with a lip more chill than stone,
   And put it in her bosom, where it dries
And freezes utterly unto the bone
   Those dainties made to still an infant's cries :
Then 'gan she work again ; nor stay'd her care,   375
But to throw back at times her veiling hair.

XLVIII.

That old nurse stood beside her wondering,
   Until her heart felt pity to the core
At sight of such a dismal labouring,
   And so she kneeled, with her locks of hoar,   380
And put her lean hands to the horrid thing :
   Three hours they labour'd at this travail sore ;
At last they felt the kernel of the grave,
And Isabella did not stamp and rave.

XLIX.

Ah ! wherefore all this wormy circumstance ?   385
   Why linger at the yawning tomb so long ?
O for the gentleness of old Romance,
   The simple plaining of a minstrel's song !
Fair reader, at the old tale take a glance,
   For here, in truth, it doth not well belong   390
To speak :—O turn thee to the very tale,
And taste the music of that vision pale.

L.

With duller steel than the Perséan sword
   They cut away no formless monster's head,

But one, whose gentleness did well accord   395
   With death, as life. The ancient harps have said,
Love never dies, but lives, immortal Lord :
   If love impersonate was ever dead,
Pale Isabella kiss'd it, and low moan'd.
'Twas love ; cold,—dead indeed, but not dethron'd. 400

LI.

In anxious secrecy they took it home,
   And then the prize was all for Isabel :
She calm'd its wild hair with a golden comb,
   And all around each eye's sepulchral cell
Pointed each fringed lash ; the smeared loam   405
   With tears, as chilly as a dripping well,
She drench'd away :—and still she comb'd, and kept
Sighing all day—and still she kiss'd, and wept.

LII.

Then in a silken scarf,—sweet with the dews
   Of precious flowers pluck'd in Araby,   410
And divine liquids come with odorous ooze
   Through the cold serpent-pipe refreshfully,—
She wrapp'd it up ; and for its tomb did choose
   A garden-pot, wherein she laid it by,
And cover'd it with mould, and o'er it set   415
Sweet Basil, which her tears kept ever wet.

LIII.

And she forgot the stars, the moon, and sun,
   And she forgot the blue above the trees,
And she forgot the dells where waters run,
   And she forgot the chilly autumn breeze ;   420

She had no knowledge when the day was done,
    And the new morn she saw not : but in peace
Hung over her sweet Basil evermore,
And moisten'd it with tears unto the core.

LIV.

And so she ever fed it with thin tears,   425
    Whence thick, and green, and beautiful it grew,
So that it smelt more balmy than its peers
    Of Basil-tufts in Florence ; for it drew
Nurture besides, and life, from human fears,
    From the fast mouldering head there shut from view : 430
So that the jewel, safely casketed,
Came forth, and in perfumed leafits spread.

LV.

O Melancholy, linger here awhile !
    O Music, Music, breathe despondingly !
O Echo, Echo, from some sombre isle,   435
    Unknown, Lethean, sigh to us—O sigh !
Spirits in grief, lift up your heads, and smile ;
    Lift up your heads, sweet Spirits, heavily,
And make a pale light in your cypress glooms,
Tinting with silver wan your marble tombs.   440

LVI.

Moan hither, all ye syllables of woe,
    From the deep throat of sad Melpomene !
Through bronzed lyre in tragic order go,
    And touch the strings into a mystery ;
Sound mournfully upon the winds and low ;   445
    For simple Isabel is soon to be

Among the dead : She withers, like a palm
Cut by an Indian for its juicy balm.

LVII.

O leave the palm to wither by itself ;
　Let not quick Winter chill its dying hour !—　　450
It may not be—those Baàlites of pelf,
　Her brethren, noted the continual shower
From her dead eyes ; and many a curious elf,
　Among her kindred, wonder'd that such dower
Of youth and beauty should be thrown aside　　455
By one mark'd out to be a Noble's bride.

LVIII.

And, furthermore, her brethren wonder'd much
　Why she sat drooping by the Basil green,
And why ıt flourish'd, as by magic touch ;
　Greatly they wonder'd what the thing might mean :
They could not surely give belief, that such　　461
　A very nothing would have power to wean
Her from her own fair youth, and pleasures gay,
And even remembrance of her love's delay.

LIX.

Therefore they watch'd a tıme when they might sift　465
　This hidden whim ; and long they watch'd in vain ;
For seldom did she go to chapel-shrift,
　And seldom felt she any hunger-pain ;
And when she left, she hurried back, as swift
　As bird on wing to breast its eggs again ;　　470
And, patient as a hen-bırd, sat her there
Beside her Basil, weeping through her hair.

LX.

Yet they contriv'd to steal the Basil-pot,
  And to examine it in secret place :
The thing was vile with green and livid spot,   475
  And yet they knew it was Lorenzo's face :
The guerdon of their murder they had got,
  And so left Florence in a moment's space,
Never to turn again.—Away they went,
With blood upon their heads, to banishment.   480

LXI.

O Melancholy, turn thine eyes away !
  O Music, Music, breathe despondingly !
O Echo, Echo, on some other day,
  From isles Lethean, sigh to us—O sigh !
Spirits of grief, sing not your " Well-a-way ! "   485
  For Isabel, sweet Isabel, will die ;
Will die a death too lone and incomplete,
Now they have ta'en away her Basil sweet.

LXII.

Piteous she look'd on dead and senseless things,
  Asking for her lost Basil amorously ;   490
And with melodious chuckle in the strings
  Of her lorn voice, she oftentimes would cry
After the Pilgrim in his wanderings,
  To ask him where her Basil was ; and why
'Twas hid from her : " For cruel 'tis," said she,   495
" To steal my Basil-pot away from me."

LXIII.

And so she pin'd and so she died forlorn,
  Imploring for her Basil to the last.

No heart was there in Florence but did mourn
   In pity of her love, so overcast.   500
And a sad ditty of this story born
   From mouth to mouth through all the country pass'd :
Still is the burthen sung—" O cruelty,
To steal my Basil-pot away from me ! "

THE EVE OF ST. AGNES.

I.

St. Agnes' Eve—Ah, bitter chill it was !
The owl, for all his feathers, was a-cold ;
The hare limp'd trembling through the frozen grass,
And silent was the flock in woolly fold :
Numb were the Beadsman's fingers, while he told   5
His rosary, and while his frosted breath,
Like pious incense from a censer old,
Seem'd taking flight for heaven, without a death,
Past the sweet Virgin's picture, while his prayer he saith.

II.

His prayer he saith, this patient, holy man ;   10
Then takes his lamp, and riseth from his knees,
And back returneth, meagre, barefoot, wan,
Along the chapel aisle by slow degrees :
The sculptur'd dead, on each side, seem to freeze,
Emprison'd in black, purgatorial rails :   15
Knights, ladies, praying in dumb orat'ries,
He passeth by ; and his weak spirit fails
To think how they may ache in icy hoods and mails.

III.

Northward he turneth through a little door,
And scarce three steps, ere Music's golden tongue   20
Flatter'd to tears this aged man and poor ;

But no—already had his deathbell rung :
The joys of all his life were said and sung :
His was harsh penance on St. Agnes' Eve :
Another way he went, and soon among   25
Rough ashes sat he for his soul's reprieve,
And all night kept awake, for sinners' sake to grieve.

IV.

That ancient Beadsman heard the prelude soft ;
And so it chanc'd, for many a door was wide,
From hurry to and fro.   Soon, up aloft,   30
The silver, snarling trumpets 'gan to chide :
The level chambers, ready with their pride,
Were glowing to receive a thousand guests :
The carved angels, ever eager-ey'd,
Star'd, where upon their heads the cornice rests,   35
With hair blown back, and wings put cross-wise on their
        breasts.

V.

At length burst in the argent revelry,
With plume, tiara, and all rich array,
Numerous as shadows haunting faerily
The brain, new stuff'd, in youth, with triumphs gay   40
Of old romance.   These let us wish away,
And turn, sole-thoughted, to one Lady there,
Whose heart had brooded, all that wintry day,
On love, and wing'd St. Agnes' saintly care,
As she had heard old dames full many times declare.   45

VI.

They told her how, upon St. Agnes' Eve,
Young virgins might have visions of delight,
And soft adorings from their loves receive
Upon the honey'd middle of the night,

If ceremonies due they did aright ;   50
As, supperless to bed they must retire,
And couch supine their beauties, lily white ;
Nor look behind, nor sideways, but require
Of Heaven with upward eyes for all that they desire.

VII.

Full of this whim was thoughtful Madeline :   55
The music, yearning like a God in pain,
She scarcely heard : her maiden eyes divine,
Fix'd on the floor, saw many a sweeping train
Pass by—she heeded not at all : in vain
Came many a tiptoe, amorous cavalier,   60
And back retir'd ; not cool'd by high disdain,
But she saw not : her heart was otherwhere :
She sigh'd for Agnes' dreams, the sweetest of the year.

VIII.

She danc'd along with vague, regardless eyes,
Anxious her lips, her breathing quick and short :   65
The hallow'd hour was near at hand : she sighs
Amid the timbrels, and the throng'd resort
Of whisperers in anger, or in sport ;
'Mid looks of love, defiance, hate, and scorn,
Hoodwink'd with faery fancy ; all amort,   70
Save to St. Agnes and her lambs unshorn,
And all the bliss to be before to-morrow morn.

IX.

So, purposing each moment to retire,
She linger'd still. Meantime, across the moors,
Had come young Porphyro, with heart on fire   75
For Madeline. Beside the portal doors,
Buttress'd from moonlight, stands he, and implores

All saints to give him sight of Madeline,
But for one moment in the tedious hours,
That he might gaze and worship all unseen ;   80
Perchance speak, kneel, touch, kiss—in sooth such things
    have been.

X.

He ventures in : let no buzz'd whisper tell :
All eyes be muffled, or a hundred swords
Will storm his heart, Love's fev'rous citadel :
For him, those chambers held barbarian hordes,   85
Hyena foemen, and hot-blooded lords,
Whose very dogs would execrations howl
Against his lineage : not one breast affords
Him any mercy, in that mansion foul,
Save one old beldame, weak in body and in soul.   90

XI.

Ah, happy chance ! the aged creature came,
Shuffling along with ivory-headed wand,
To where he stood, hid from the torch's flame,
Behind a broad hall-pillar, far beyond
The sound of merriment and chorus bland :   95
He startled her ; but soon she knew his face,
And grasp'd his fingers in her palsied hand,
Saying, " Mercy, Porphyro ! hie thee from this place ;
They are all here to-night, the whole blood-thirsty race !

XII.

Get hence ! get hence ! there's dwarfish Hildebrand ; 100
He had a fever late, and in the fit
He cursed thee and thine, both house and land :
Then there's that old Lord Maurice, not a whit
More tame for his gray hairs—Alas me ! flit !

Flit like a ghost away."—" Ah, Gossip dear,   105
We're safe enough , here in this arm-chair sit,
And tell me how "—" Good Saints ! not here, not here ;
Follow me, child, or else these stones will be thy bier."

XIII.

He follow'd through a lowly arched way,
Brushing the cobwebs with his lofty plume,   110
And as she mutter'd " Well-a—well-a-day ! "
He found him in a little moonlight room,
Pale, lattic'd, chill, and silent as a tomb.
Now tell me where is Madeline," said he,
O tell me, Angela, by the holy loom   115
Which none but secret sisterhood may see,
When they St. Agnes' wool are weaving piously."

XIV.

" St. Agnes ! Ah ! it is St. Agnes' Eve—
Yet men will murder upon holy days :
Thou must hold water in a witch's sieve,   120
And be liege-lord of all the Elves and Fays,
To venture so : it fills me with amaze
To see thee, Porphyro !—St. Agnes' Eve !
God's help ! my lady fair the conjuror plays
This very night : good angels her deceive !   125
But let me laugh awhile, I've mickle time to grieve."

XV.

Feebly she laugheth in the languid moon,
While Porphyro upon her face doth look,
Like puzzled urchin on an aged crone
Who keepeth clos'd a wond'rous riddle-book,   130
As spectacled she sits in chimney nook.
But soon his eyes grew brilliant, when she told

His lady's purpose ; and he scarce could brook
Tears, at the thought of those enchantments cold,
And Madeline asleep in lap of legends old.   135

XVI.

Sudden a thought came like a full-blown rose,
Flushing his brow, and in his pained heart
Made purple riot : then doth he propose
A stratagem, that makes the beldame start :
" A cruel man and impious thou art :   140
Sweet lady, let her pray, and sleep, and dream
Alone with her good angels, far apart
From wicked men like thee.   Go, go !—I deem
Thou canst not surely be the same that thou didst seem."

XVII.

" I will not harm her, by all saints I swear,"   145
Quoth Porphyro : " O may I ne'er find grace
When my weak voice shall whisper its last prayer,
If one of her soft ringlets I displace,
Or look with ruffian passion in her face :
Good Angela, believe me by these tears ;   150
Or I will, even in a moment's space,
Awake with horrid shout, my foemen's ears,
And beard them, though they be more fang'd than wolves
    and bears."

XVIII.

" Ah ! why wilt thou affright a feeble soul ?
A poor, weak, palsy-stricken, churchyard thing,   155
Whose passing-bell may ere the midnight toll ;
Whose prayers for thee, each morn and evening,
Were never miss'd."—Thus plaining, doth she bring
A gentler speech from burning Porphyro ;

So woeful, and of such deep sorrowing,   160
That Angela gives promise she will do
Whatever he shall wish, betide her weal or woe.

XIX.

Which was, to lead him, in close secrecy,
Even to Madeline's chamber, and there hide
Him in a closet, of such privacy   165
That he might see her beauty unespy'd,
And win perhaps that night a peerless bride,
While legion'd faeries pac'd the coverlet,   .
And pale enchantment held her sleepy-ey'd.
Never on such a night have lovers met,   170
Since Merlin paid his Demon all the monstrous debt.

XX.

" It shall be as thou wishest," said the Dame :
" All cates and dainties shall be stored there
Quickly on this feast-night : by the tambour frame
Her own lute thou wilt see : no time to spare,   175
For I am slow and feeble, and scarce dare
On such a catering trust my dizzy head.
Wait here, my child, with patience ; kneel in prayer
The while : Ah ! thou must needs the lady wed,
Or may I never leave my grave among the dead."   180

XXI.

So saying, she hobbled off with busy fear.
The lover's endless minutes slowly pass'd ;
The dame return'd, and whisper'd in his ear
To follow her ; with aged eyes aghast
From fright of dim espial. Safe at last,   185
Through many a dusky gallery, they gain

The maiden's chamber, silken, hush'd, and chaste ;
Where Porphyro took covert, pleas'd amain.
His poor guide hurried back with agues in her brain.

XXII.

Her falt'ring hand upon the balustrade,   190
Old Angela was feeling for the stair,
When Madeline, St. Agnes' charmed maid,
Rose, like a mission'd spirit, unaware :
With silver taper's light, and pious care,
She turn'd, and down the aged gossip led   195
To a safe level matting.   Now prepare,
Young Porphyro, for gazing on that bed ;
She comes, she comes again, like ring-dove fray'd and fled.

XXIII.

Out went the taper as she hurried in ;
Its little smoke, in pallid moonshine, died :   200
She clos'd the door, she panted, all akin
To spirits of the air, and visions wide :
No uttered syllable, or, woe betide !
But to her heart, her heart was voluble,
Paining with eloquence her balmy side ;   205
As though a tongueless nightingale should swell
Her throat in vain, and die, heart-stifled, in her dell.

XXIV.

A casement high and triple-arch'd there was,
All garlanded with carven imag'ries
Of fruits, and flowers, and bunches of knot-grass,   210
And diamonded with panes of quaint device,
Innumerable of stains and splendid dyes,
As are the tiger-moth's deep-damask'd wings ;

And in the midst, 'mong thousand heraldries,
And twilight saints, and dim emblazonings,   215
A shielded scutcheon blush'd with blood of queens and kings.

XXV.

Full on this casement shone the wintry moon,
And threw warm gules on Madeline's fair breast,
As down she knelt for heaven's grace and boon ;
Rose-bloom fell on her hands, together prest,   220
And on her silver cross soft amethyst,
And on her hair a glory, like a saint :
She seem'd a splendid angel, newly drest,
Save wings, for heaven :—Porphyro grew faint :
She knelt, so pure a thing, so free from mortal taint.   225

XXVI.

Anon his heart revives : her vespers done,
Of all its wreathed pearls her hair she frees ;
Unclasps her warmed jewels one by one ;
Loosens her fragrant boddice; by degrees
Her rich attire creeps rustling to her knees :   230
Half-hidden, like a mermaid in sea-weed,
Pensive awhile she dreams awake, and sees,
In fancy, fair St. Agnes in her bed,
But dares not look behind, or all the charm is fled.

XXVII.

Soon, trembling in her soft and chilly nest,   235
In sort of wakeful swoon, perplex'd she lay,
Until the poppied warmth of sleep oppress'd
Her soothed limbs, and soul fatigued away ;
Flown, like a thought, until the morrow-day ;
Blissfully haven'd both from joy and pain ;
Clasp'd like a missal where swart Paynims pray ;   240

Blinded alike from sunshine and from rain,
As though a rose should shut, and be a bud again.

XXVIII.

Stol'n to this paradise, and so entranced,
Porphyro gaz'd upon her empty dress,   245
And listen'd to her breathing, if it chanced
To wake into a slumberous tenderness ;
Which when he heard, that minute did he bless,
And breath'd himself : then from the closet crept,
Noiseless as fear in a wide wilderness,   250
And over the hush'd carpet, silent, stept,
And 'tween the curtains peep'd, where, lo !—how fast she
    slept.

XXIX.

Then by the bed-side, where the faded moon
Made a dim, silver twilight, soft he set
A table, and, half anguish'd, threw thereon   255
A cloth of woven crimson, gold, and jet :—
O for some drowsy Morphean amulet !
The boisterous, midnight, festive clarion,
The kettle-drum, and far-heard clarinet,
Affray his ears, though but in dying tone :—   260
The hall door shuts again, and all the noise is gone.

XXX.

And still she slept an azure-lidded sleep,
In blanched linen, smooth, and lavender'd,
While he from forth the closet brought a heap
Of candied apple, quince, and plum, and gourd ,   265
With jellies soother than the creamy curd,
And lucent syrops, tinct with cinnamon ;
Manna and dates, in argosy transferr'd

From Fez ; and spiced dainties, every one,
From silken Samarcand to cedar'd Lebanon.   270

XXXI.

These delicates he heap'd with glowing hand
On golden dishes and in baskets bright
Of wreathed silver : sumptuous they stand
In the retired quiet of the night,
Filling the chilly room with perfume light.—   275
" And now, my love, my seraph fair, awake !
Thou art my heaven, and I thine eremite :
Open thine eyes, for meek St. Agnes' sake,
Or I shall drowse beside thee, so my soul doth ache."

XXXII.

Thus whispering, his warm, unnerved arm   280
Sank in her pillow.   Shaded was her dream
By the dusk curtains :—'twas a midnight charm
Impossible to melt as iced stream :
The lustrous salvers in the moonlight gleam ;
Broad golden fringe upon the carpet lies :   285
It seem'd he never, never could redeem
From such a stedfast spell his lady's eyes ;
So mus'd awhile, entoil'd in woofed phantasies.

XXXIII.

Awakening up, he took her hollow lute,—
Tumultuous,—and, in chords that tenderest be,   290
He play'd an ancient ditty, long since mute,
In Provence call'd, " La belle dame sans mercy : "
Close to her ear touching the melody ;—
Wherewith disturb'd, she utter'd a soft moan :
He ceas'd—she panted quick—and suddenly   295

Her blue affrayed eyes wide open shone :
Upon his knees he sank, pale as smooth-sculptured stone.

XXXIV.

Her eyes were open, but she still beheld,
Now wide awake, the vision of her sleep :
There was a painful change, that nigh expell'd   300
The blisses of her dream so pure and deep
At which fair Madeline began to weep,
And moan forth witless words with many a sigh ;
While still her gaze on Porphyro would keep ;
Who knelt, with joined hands and piteous eye,   305
Fearing to move or speak, she look'd so dreamingly.

XXXV.

" Ah, Porphyro ! " said she, " but even now
Thy voice was at sweet tremble in mine ear,
Made tuneable with every sweetest vow ;
And those sad eyes were spiritual and clear :   310
How chang'd thou art ! how pallid, chill, and drear !
Give me that voice again, my Porphyro,
Those looks immortal, those complainings dear !
Oh leave me not in this eternal woe,
For if thou diest, my Love, I know not where to go." 315

XXXVI.

Beyond a mortal man impassion'd far
At these voluptuous accents, he arose,
Ethereal, flush'd, and like a throbbing star
Seen mid the sapphire heaven's deep repose ;
Into her dream he melted, as the rose   320
Blendeth its odour with the violet,—
Solution sweet : meantime the frost-wind blows
Like Love's alarum pattering the sharp sleet
Against the window-panes ; St. Agnes' moon hath set.

XXXVII.

'Tis dark : quick pattereth the flaw-blown sleet :   325
" This is no dream, my bride, my Madeline ! "
'Tis dark : the iced gusts still rave and beat :
" No dream, alas ! alas ! and woe is mine !
Porphyro will leave me here to fade and pine.—
Cruel ! what traitor could thee hither bring ?   330
I curse not, for my heart is lost in thine,
Though thou forsakest a deceived thing ;—
A dove forlorn and lost with sick unpruned wing."

XXXVIII.

" My Madeline ! sweet dreamer ! lovely bride !
Say, may I be for aye thy vassal blest ?   335
Thy beauty's shield, heart-shap'd and vermeil dy'd ?
Ah, silver shrine, here will I take my rest
After so many hours of toil and quest,
A famish'd pilgrim,—sav'd by miracle.
Though I have found, I will not rob thy nest   340
Saving of thy sweet self ; if thou think'st well
To trust, fair Madeline, to no rude infidel.

XXXIX.

Hark ! 'tis an elfin-storm from faery land,
Of haggard seeming, but a boon indeed :
Arise—arise ! the morning is at hand ;—   345
The bloated wassaillers will never heed :—
Let us away, my love, with happy speed ;
There are no ears to hear, or eyes to see,—
Drown'd all in Rhenish and the sleepy mead :
Awake ! arise ! my love, and fearless be,   350
For o'er the southern moors I have a home for thee."

XL.

She hurried at his words, beset with fears,
For there were sleeping dragons all around,
At glaring watch, perhaps, with ready spears—
Down the wide stairs a darkling way they found.—   355
In all the house was heard no human sound.
A chain-droop'd lamp was flickering by each door ;
The arras, rich with horsemen, hawk, and hound,
Flutter'd in the besieging wind's uproar ;
And the long carpets rose along the gusty floor.   360

XLI.

They glide, like phantoms, into the wide hall ;
Like phantoms, to the iron porch, they glide ;
Where lay the Porter, in uneasy sprawl,
With a huge empty flaggon by his side :
The wakeful bloodhound rose, and shook his hide,   365
But his sagacious eye an inmate owns :
By one, and one, the bolts full easy slide :—
The chains lie silent on the footworn stones ;—
The key turns, and the door upon its hinges groans.

XLII.

And they are gone : aye, ages long ago   370
These lovers fled away into the storm.
That night the Baron dreamt of many a woe,
And all his warrior-guests, with shade and form
Of witch, and demon, and large coffin-worm,
Were long be-nightmar'd.   Angela the old   375
Died palsy-twitch'd, with meagre face deform ;
The Beadsman, after thousand aves told,
For aye unsought for slept among his ashes cold.

LAMIA.

PART I.

Upon a time, before the faery broods
Drove Nymph and Satyr from the prosperous woods,
Before King Oberon's bright diadem,
Sceptre, and mantle, clasp'd with dewy gem,
Frighted away the Dryads and the Fauns   5
From rushes green, and brakes, and cowslip'd lawns,
The ever-smitten Hermes empty left
His golden throne, bent warm on amorous theft :
From high Olympus had he stolen light,
On this side of Jove's clouds, to escape the sight   10
Of his great summoner, and made retreat
Into a forest on the shores of Crete.
For somewhere in that sacred island dwelt
A nymph, to whom all hoofed Satyrs knelt ;
At whose white feet the languid Tritons poured   15
Pearls, while on land they wither'd and adored.
Fast by the springs where she to bathe was wont,
And in those meads where sometime she might haunt,
Were strewn rich gifts, unknown to any Muse,
Though Fancy's casket were unlock'd to choose.   20
Ah, what a world of love was at her feet !
So Hermes thought, and a celestial heat
Burnt from his winged heels to either ear,
That from a whiteness, as the lily clear,
Blush'd into roses 'mid his golden hair,   25
Fallen in jealous curls about his shoulders bare.

From vale to vale, from wood to wood, he flew,
Breathing upon the flowers his passion new,
And wound with many a river to its head,
To find where this sweet nymph prepar'd her secret bed :
In vain ; the sweet nymph might nowhere be found,　　31
And so he rested, on the lonely ground,
Pensive, and full of painful jealousies
Of the Wood-Gods, and even the very trees.
There as he stood, he heard a mournful voice,　　35
Such as once heard, in gentle heart, destroys
All pain but pity : thus the lone voice spake :
" When from this wreathed tomb shall I awake !
When move in a sweet body fit for life,
And love, and pleasure, and the ruddy strife　　40
Of hearts and lips ! Ah, miserable me ! "
The God, dove-footed, glided silently
Round bush and tree, soft-brushing, in his speed,
The taller grasses and full-flowering weed,
Until he found a palpitating snake,　　45
Bright, and cirque-couchant in a dusky brake.

She was a gordian shape of dazzling hue,
Vermillion-spotted, golden, green, and blue ;
Strip'd like a zebra, freckled like a pard,
Ey'd like a peacock, and all crimson barr'd ;　　50
And full of silver moons, that, as she breathed,
Dissolv'd, or brighter shone, or interwreathed
Their lustres with the gloomier tapestries—
So rainbow-sided, touch'd with miseries,
She seem'd, at once, some penanc'd lady elf,　　55
Some demon's mistress, or the demon's self.
Upon her crest she wore a wannish fire
Sprinkled with stars, like Ariadne's tiar :
Her head was serpent, but ah, bitter-sweet !
She had a woman's mouth with all its pearls complete :　　60

And for her eyes : what could such eyes do there
But weep, and weep, that they were born so fair ?
As Proserpine still weeps for her Silician air.
Her throat was serpent, but the words she spake
Came, as through bubbling honey, for Love's sake,   65
And thus ; while Hermes on his pinions lay,
Like a stoop'd falcon ere he takes his prey.

  " Fair Hermes, crown'd with feathers, fluttering light,
I had a splendid dream of thee last night :
I saw thee sitting, on a throne of gold,   70
Among the Gods, upon Olympus old,
The only sad one ; for thou didst not hear
The soft, lute-finger'd Muses chaunting clear,
Nor even Apollo when he sang alone,
Deaf to his throbbing throat's long, long melodious moan. 75
I dreamt I saw thee, rob'd in purple flakes,
Break amorous through the clouds, as morning breaks,
And, swiftly as a bright Phoebean dart,
Strike for the Cretan isle ; and here thou art !
Too gentle Hermes, hast thou found the maid ? "   80
Whereat the star of Lethe not delay'd
His rosy eloquence, and thus inquired :
" Thou smooth-lipp'd serpent, surely high inspired !
Thou beauteous wreath, with melancholy eyes,
Possess whatever bliss thou canst devise,   85
Telling me only where my nymph is fled,—
Where she doth breathe ! " " Bright planet, thou hast
    said,"
Return'd the snake, " but seal with oaths, fair God ! "
" I swear," said Hermes, " by my serpent rod,
And by thine eyes, and by thy starry crown ! "   90
Light flew his earnest words, among the blossoms blown.
Then thus again the brilliance feminine :
" Too frail of heart ! for this lost nymph of thine,

Free as the air, invisibly, she strays
About these thornless wilds ; her pleasant days   95
She tastes unseen ; unseen her nimble feet
Leave traces in the grass and flowers sweet ;
From weary tendrils, and bow'd branches green,
She plucks the fruit unseen, she bathes unseen :
And by my power is her beauty veil'd   100
To keep it unaffronted, unassail'd
By the love-glances of unlovely eyes,
Of Satyrs, Fauns, and blear'd Silenus' sights.
Pale grew her immortality, for woe
Of all these lovers, and she grieved so   105
I took compassion on her, bade her steep
Her hair in weird syrops, that would keep
Her loveliness invisible, yet free
To wander as she loves, in liberty.
Thou shalt behold her, Hermes, thou alone,   110
If thou wilt, as thou swearest, grant my boon ! ''
Then, once again, the charmed God began
An oath, and through the serpent's ears it ran
Warm, tremulous, devout, psalterian.
Ravish'd, she lifted her Circean head,   115
Blush'd a live damask, and swift-lisping said,
'' I was a woman, let me have once more
A woman's shape, and charming as before.
I love a youth of Corinth—O the bliss !
Give me my woman's form, and place me where he is.   120
Stoop, Hermes, let me breathe upon thy brow,
And thou shalt see thy sweet nymph even now.''
The God on half-shut feathers sank serene,
She breath'd upon his eyes, and swift was seen
Of both the guarded nymph near-smiling on the green. 125
It was no dream ; or say a dream it was,
Real are the dreams of Gods, and smoothly pass
Their pleasures in a long immortal dream.

One warm, flush'd moment, hovering, it might seem
Dash'd by the wood-nymph's beauty, so he burn'd ;   130
Then, lighting on the printless verdure, turn'd
To the swoon'd serpent, and with languid arm,
Delicate, put to proof the lythe Caducean charm.
So done, upon the nymph his eyes he bent
Full of adoring tears and blandishment,   135
And towards her stept . she, like a moon in wane,
Faded before him, cower'd, nor could restrain
Her fearful sobs, self-folding like a flower
That faints into itself at evening hour :
But the God fostering her chilled hand,   140
She felt the warmth, her eyelids open'd bland,
And, like new flowers at morning song of bees,
Bloom'd, and gave up her honey to the lees.
Into the green-recessed woods they flew ;
Nor grew they pale, as mortal lovers do.   145

   Left to herself, the serpent now began
To change ; her elfin blood in madness ran,
Her mouth foam'd, and the grass, therewith besprent,
Wither'd at dew so sweet and virulent ;
Her eyes in torture fix'd, and anguish drear,   150
Hot, glaz'd, and wide, with lid-lashes all sear,
Flash'd phosphor and sharp sparks, without one cooling tear.
The colours all inflam'd throughout her train,
She writh'd about, convuls'd with scarlet pain :
A deep volcanian yellow took the place   155
Of all her milder-mooned body's grace ;
And, as the lava ravishes the mead,
Spoilt all her silver mail, and golden brede ;
Made gloom of all her frecklings, streaks and bars,
Eclips'd her crescents, and lick'd up her stars :   160
So that, in moments few, she was undrest
Of all her sapphires, greens, and amethyst,

And rubious-argent : of all these bereft,
Nothing but pain and ugliness were left.
Still shone her crown ; that vanish'd, also she   165
Melted and disappear'd as suddenly ;
And in the air, her new voice luting soft,
Cry'd, " Lycius ! gentle Lycius ! "—Borne aloft
With the bright mists about the mountains hoar
These words dissolv'd : Crete's forests heard no more.   170

    Whither fled Lamia, now a lady bright,
A full-born beauty new and exquisite ?
She fled into that valley they pass o'er
Who go to Corinth from Cenchreas' shore ;
And rested at the foot of those wild hills,   175
The rugged founts of the Peraean rills,
And of that other ridge whose barren back
Stretches, with all its mist and cloudy rack,
South-westward to Cleone.   There she stood
About a young bird's flutter from a wood,   180
Fair, on a sloping green of mossy tread,
By a clear pool, wherein she passioned
To see herself escap'd from so sore ills,
While her robes flaunted with the daffodils.

    Ah, happy Lycius !—for she was a maid   185
More beautiful than ever twisted braid,
Or sigh'd, or blush'd, or on spring-flowered lea
Spread a green kirtle to the minstrelsy :
A virgin purest lipp'd, yet in the lore
Of love deep learned to the red heart's core :   190
Not one hour old, yet of sciential brain
To unperplex bliss from its neighbour pain ;
Define their pettish limits, and estrange
Their points of contact, and swift counterchange ;
Intrigue with the specious chaos, and dispart   195

Its most ambiguous atoms with sure art ;
As though in Cupid's college she had spent
Sweet days a lovely graduate, still unshent,
And kept his rosy terms in idle languishment.

Why this fair creature chose so faerily 200
By the wayside to linger, we shall see ;
But first 'tis fit to tell how she could muse
And dream, when in the serpent prison-house,
Of all she list, strange or magnificent :
How, ever, where she will'd, her spirit went ; 205
Whether to faint Elysium, or where
Down through tress-lifting waves the Nereids fair
Wind into Thetis' bower by many a pearly stair ;
Or where God Bacchus drains his cups divine,
Stretch'd out, at ease, beneath a glutinous pine ; 210
Or where in Pluto's gardens palatine
Mulciber's columns gleam in far piazzian line.
And sometimes into cities she would send
Her dream, with feast and rioting to blend ;
And once, while among mortals dreaming thus, 215
She saw the young Corinthian Lycius
Charioting foremost in the envious race,
Like a young Jove with calm uneager face,
And fell into a swooning love of him.
Now on the moth-time of that evening dim 220
He would return that way, as well she knew,
To Corinth from the shore ; for freshly blew
The eastern soft wind, and his galley now
Grated the quaystones with her brazen prow
In port Cenchreas, from Egina isle 225
Fresh anchor'd ; whither he had been awhile
To sacrifice to Jove, whose temple there
Waits with high marble doors of blood and incense rare.
Jove heard his vows, and better'd his desire ;

KTS. 6

For by some freakful chance he made retire   230
From his companions, and set forth to walk,
Perhaps grown wearied of their Corinth talk :
Over the solitary hills he fared,
Thoughtless at first, but ere eve's star appeared
His phantasy was lost, where reason fades,   235
In the calm'd twilight of Platonic shades.
Lamia beheld him coming, near, more near—
Close to her passing, in indifference drear,
His silent sandals swept the mossy green ;
So neighbour'd to him, and yet so unseen   240
She stood : he pass'd, shut up in mysteries,
His mind wrapp'd like his mantle, while her eyes
Follow'd his steps, and her neck regal white
Turn'd—syllabling thus, " Ah, Lycius bright,
And will you leave me on the hills alone ?   245
Lycius, look back ! and be some pity shown."
He did ; not with cold wonder fearingly,
But Orpheus-like at an Eurydice ;
For so delicious were the words she sung,
It seem'd he had lov'd them a whole summer long :   250
And soon his eyes had drunk her beauty up,
Leaving no drop in the bewildering cup,
And still the cup was full,—while he, afraid
Lest she should vanish ere his lip had paid
Due adoration, thus began to adore ;   255
Her soft look growing coy, she saw his chain so sure :
" Leave thee alone ! Look back ! Ah, Goddess, see
Whether my eyes can ever turn from thee !
For pity do not this sad heart belie—
Even as thou vanishest so shall I die.   260
Stay ! though a Naiad of the rivers, stay !
To thy far wishes will thy streams obey :
Stay ! though the greenest woods be thy domain,
Alone they can drink up the morning rain :

Though a descended Pleiad, will not one 265
Of thine harmonious sisters keep in tune
Thy spheres, and as thy silver proxy shine?
So sweetly to these ravish'd ears of mine
Came thy sweet greeting, that if thou shouldst fade
Thy memory will waste me to a shade :— 270
For pity do not melt!"—"If I should stay,"
Said Lamia, "here, upon this floor of clay,
And pain my steps upon these flowers too rough,
What canst thou say or do of charm enough
To dull the nice remembrance of my home? 275
Thou canst not ask me with thee here to roam
Over these hills and vales, where no joy is,—
Empty of immortality and bliss!
Thou art a scholar, Lycius, and must know
That finer spirits cannot breathe below 280
In human climes, and live : Alas! poor youth,
What taste of purer air hast thou to soothe
My essence? What serener palaces,
Where I may all my many senses please,
And by mysterious sleights a hundred thirsts appease? 285
It cannot be—Adieu!" So said, she rose
Tiptoe with white arms spread. He, sick to lose
The amorous promise of her lone complain,
Swoon'd, murmuring of love, and pale with pain.
The cruel lady, without any show 290
Of sorrow for her tender favourite's woe,
But rather, if her eyes could brighter be,
With brighter eyes and slow amenity,
Put her new lips to his, and gave afresh
The life she had so tangled in her mesh : 295
And as he from one trance was wakening
Into another, she began to sing,
Happy in beauty, life, and love, and every thing,
A song of love, too sweet for earthly lyres,

While, like held breath, the stars drew in their panting fires.
And then she whisper'd in such trembling tone,   301
As those who, safe together met alone
For the first time through many anguish'd days,
Use other speech than looks ; bidding him raise
His drooping head, and clear his soul of doubt,   305
For that she was a woman, and without
Any more subtle fluid in her veins
Than throbbing blood, and that the self-same pains
Inhabited her frail-strung heart as his.
And next she wonder'd how his eyes could miss   310
Her face so long in Corinth, where, she said,
She dwelt but half retir'd, and there had led
Days happy as the gold coin could invent
Without the aid of love ; yet in content
Till she saw him, as once she pass'd him by,   315
Where 'gainst a column he leant thoughtfully
At Venus' temple porch, 'mid baskets heap'd
Of amorous herbs and flowers, newly reap'd
Late on that eve, as 'twas the night before
The Adonian feast ; whereof she saw no more,   320
But wept alone those days, for why should she adore ?
Lycius from death awoke into amaze,
To see her still, and singing so sweet lays ;
Then from amaze into delight he fell
To hear her whisper woman's lore so well ;   325
And every word she spake entic'd him on
To unperplex'd delight and pleasure known.
Let the mad poets say whate'er they please
Of the sweets of Faeries, Peris, Goddesses,
There is not such a treat among them all,   330
Haunters of cavern, lake, and waterfall,
As a real woman, lineal indeed
From Pyrrha's pebbles or old Adam's seed.
Thus gentle Lamia judg'd, and judg'd aright,

That Lycius could not love in half a fright,   335
So threw the goddess off, and won his heart
More pleasantly by playing woman's part,
With no more awe than what her beauty gave,
That, while it smote, still guaranteed to save.
Lycius to all made eloquent reply,   340
Marrying to every word a twinborn sigh ;
And last, pointing to Corinth, ask'd her sweet,
If 'twas too far that night for her soft feet.
The way was short, for Lamia's eagerness
Made, by a spell, the triple league decrease   345
To a few paces ; not at all surmised
By blinded Lycius, so in her comprized.
They pass'd the city gates, he knew not how,
So noiseless, and he never thought to know.

    As men talk in a dream, so Corinth all,   350
Throughout her palaces imperial,
And all her populous streets and temples lewd,
Mutter'd, like tempest in the distance brew'd,
To the wide-spreaded night above her towers.
Men, women, rich and poor, in the cool hours,   355
Shuffled their sandals o'er the pavement white,
Companion'd or alone ; while many a light
Flar'd, here and there, from wealthy festivals,
And threw their moving shadows on the walls,
Or found them cluster'd in the cornic'd shade   360
Of some arch'd temple door, or dusky colonnade.

    Muffling his face, of greeting friends in fear,
Her fingers he press'd hard, as one came near
With curl'd gray beard, sharp eyes, and smooth bald crown,
Slow-stepp'd, and rob'd in philosophic gown :   365
Lycius shrank closer, as they met and past,
Into his mantle, adding wings to haste,

While hurried Lamia trembled : " Ah," said he,
" Why do you shudder love, so ruefully ?
Why does your tender palm dissolve in dew ? "—   370
" I'm wearied," said fair Lamia : " tell me who
Is that old man ? I cannot bring to mind
His features :—Lycius ! wherefore did you blind
Yourself from his quick eyes ? " Lycius reply'd,
" 'Tis Apollonius sage, my trusty guide   375
And good instructor ; but to-night he seems
The ghost of folly haunting my sweet dreams."

    While yet he spake they had arriv'd before
A pillar'd porch, with lofty portal door,
Where hung a silver lamp, whose phosphor glow   380
Reflected in the slabbed steps below,
Mild as a star in water ; for so new,
And so unsully'd was the marble's hue,
So through the crystal polish, liquid fine,
Ran the dark veins, that none but feet divine   385
Could e'er have touch'd there. Sounds Aeolian
Breath'd from the hinges, as the ample span
Of the wide doors disclos'd a place unknown
Some time to any, but those two alone,
And a few Persian mutes, who that same year   390
Were seen about the markets : none knew where
They could inhabit ; the most curious
Were foil'd, who watch'd to trace them to their house :
And but the flitter-winged verse must tell,
For truth's sake, what woe afterwards befel,   395
'Twould humour many a heart to leave them thus,
Shut from the busy world of more incredulous.

PART II.

Love in a hut, with water and a crust,
Is—Love, forgive us !—cinders, ashes, dust ;
Love in a palace is perhaps at last
More grievous torment than a hermit's fast :—
That is a doubtful tale from faery land,   5
Hard for the non-elect to understand.
Had Lycius liv'd to hand his story down,
He might have given the moral a fresh frown,
Or clench'd it quite : but too short was their bliss
To breed distrust and hate, that make the soft voice hiss. 10
Besides, there, nightly, with terrific glare,
Love, jealous grown of so complete a pair,
Hover'd and buzz'd his wings, with fearful roar,
Above the lintel of their chamber door,
And down the passage cast a glow upon the floor.   15

   For all this came a ruin : side by side
They were enthroned, in the even tide,
Upon a couch, near to a curtaining
Whose airy texture, from a golden string,
Floated into the room, and let appear   20
Unveil'd the summer heaven, blue and clear,
Betwixt two marble shafts :—there they reposed,
Where use had made it sweet, with eyelids closed,
Saving a tythe which love still open kept,
That they might see each other while they almost slept ; 25
When from the slope side of a suburb hill,
Deafening the swallow's twitter, came a thrill
Of trumpets—Lycius startled—the sounds fled,

But left a thought, a buzzing in his head.
For the first time, since first he harbour'd in   30
That purple-lined palace of sweet sin,
His spirit pass'd beyond its golden bourn
Into the noisy world almost forsworn.
The lady, ever watchful, penetrant,
Saw this with pain, so arguing a want   35
Of something more, more than her empery
Of joys ; and she began to moan and sigh
Because he mus'd beyond her, knowing well
That but a moment's thought is passion's passing bell.
" Why do you sigh, fair creature ? " whisper'd he :   40
" Why do you think ? " return'd she tenderly :
" You have deserted me ;—where am I now ?
" Not in your heart while care weighs on your brow :
No, no, you have dismiss'd me ; and I go
From your breast houseless : aye, it must be so."   45
He answer'd, bending to her open eyes,
Where he was mirror'd small in paradise,
" My silver planet, both of eve and morn !
Why will you plead yourself so sad forlorn,
While I am striving how to fill my heart   50
With deeper crimson, and a double smart ?
How to entangle, trammel up and snare
Your soul in mine, and labyrinth you there
Like the hid scent in an unbudded rose ?
Aye, a sweet kiss—you see your mighty woes.   55
My thoughts ! shall I unveil them ?   Listen then !
What mortal hath a prize, that other men
May be confounded and abash'd withal,
But lets it sometimes pace abroad majestical,
And triumph, as in thee I should rejoice   60
Amid the hoarse alarm of Corinth's voice.
Let my foes choke, and my friends shout afar,
While through the thronged streets your bridal car

Wheels round its dazzling spokes."—The lady's cheek
Trembled ; she nothing said, but, pale and meek,   65
Arose and knelt before him, wept a rain
Of sorrows at his words ; at last with pain
Beseeching him, the while his hand she wrung,
To change his purpose.   He thereat was stung,
Perverse, with stronger fancy to reclaim   70
Her wild and timid nature to his aim :
Besides, for all his love, in self despite,
Against his better self, he took delight
Luxurious in her sorrows, soft and new.
His passion, cruel grown, took on a hue   75
Fierce and sanguineous as 'twas possible
In one whose brow had no dark veins to swell.
Fine was the mitigated fury, like
Apollo's presence when in act to strike
The serpent—Ha, the serpent ! certes, she   80
Was none. She burnt, she lov'd the tyranny,
And, all subdu'd, consented to the hour
When to the bridal he should lead his paramour.
Whispering in midnight silence, said the youth,
" Sure some sweet name thou hast, though, by my truth, 85
I have not ask'd it, ever thinking thee
Not mortal, but of heavenly progeny,
As still I do.   Hast any mortal name,
Fit appellation for this dazzling frame ?
Or friends or kinsfolk on the cited earth,   90
To share our marriage feast and nuptial mirth ? "
" I have no friends," said Lamia, " no, not one ;
My presence in wide Corinth hardly known :
My parents' bones are in their dusty urns
Sepulchred, where no kindled incense burns,   95
Seeing all their luckless race are dead, save me,
And I neglect the holy rite for thee.
Even as you list invite your many guests ;

But if, as now it seems, your vision rests
With any pleasure on me, do not bid   100
Old Apollonius—from him keep me hid."
Lycius, perplex'd at words so blind and blank,
Made close inquiry ; from whose touch she shrank,
Feigning a sleep ; and he to the dull shade
Of deep sleep in a moment was betray'd.   105

   It was the custom then to bring away
The bride from home at blushing shut of day,
Veil'd, in a chariot, heralded along
By strewn flowers, torches, and a marriage song,
With other pageants : but this fair unknown   110
Had not a friend.   So being left alone,
(Lycius was gone to summon all his kin)
And knowing surely she could never win
His foolish heart from its mad pompousness,
She set herself, high-thoughted, how to dress   115
The misery in fit magnificence.
She did so, but 'tis doubtful how and whence
Came, and who were her subtle servitors.
About the halls, and to and from the doors,
There was a noise of wings, till in short space   120
The glowing banquet-room shone with wide-arched grace.
A haunting music, sole perhaps and lone
Supportress of the faery-roof, made moan
Throughout, as fearful the whole charm might fade.
Fresh carved cedar, mimicking a glade   125
Of palm and plantain, met from either side,
High in the midst, in honor of the bride :
Two palms and then two plantains, and so on,
From either side their stems branch'd one to one
All down the aisled place ; and beneath all   130
There ran a stream of lamps straight on from wall to wall.
So canopy'd, lay an untasted feast

Teeming with odours.   Lamia, regal drest,
Silently pac'd about, and as she went,
In pale contented sort of discontent,   135
Mission'd her viewless servants to enrich
The fretted splendour of each nook and niche.
Between the tree-stems, marbled plain at first,
Came jasper pannels ; then, anon, there burst
Forth creeping imagery of slighter trees,   140
And with the large wove in small intricacies.
Approving all, she faded at self-will,
And shut the chamber up, close, hush'd and still,
Complete and ready for the revels rude,
When dreadful guests would come to spoil her solitude. 145

   The day appear'd, and all the gossip rout.
O senseless Lycius ! Madman ! wherefore flout
The silent-blessing fate, warm cloister'd hours,
And show to common eyes these secret bowers ?
The herd approach'd ; each guest, with busy brain,   150
Arriving at the portal, gaz'd amain,
And enter'd marveling : for they knew the street,
Remember'd it from childhood all complete
Without a gap, yet ne'er before had seen
That royal porch, that high-built fair demesne ;   155
So in they hurried all, maz'd, curious and keen :
Save one, who look'd thereon with eye severe,
And with calm-planted steps walk'd in austere ;
'Twas Apollonius : something too he laugh'd,
As though some knotty problem, that had daft   160
His patient thought, had now begun to thaw,
And solve and melt :—'twas just as he foresaw.

   He met within the murmurous vestibule
His young disciple. " 'Tis no common rule,
Lycius," said he, " for uninvited guest   165

To force himself upon you, and infest
With an unbidden presence the bright throng
Of younger friends ; yet must I do this wrong,
And you forgive me."   Lycius blush'd, and led
The old man through the inner doors broad-spread ;   170
With reconciling words and courteous mien
Turning into sweet milk the sophist's spleen.

   Of wealthy lustre was the banquet-room,
Fill'd with pervading brilliance and perfume :
Before each lucid pannel fuming stood   175
A censer fed with myrrh and spiced wood,
Each by a sacred tripod held aloft,
Whose slender feet wide-swerv'd upon the soft
Wool-woofed carpets : fifty wreaths of smoke
From fifty censers their light voyage took   180
To the high roof, still mimick'd as they rose
Along the mirror'd walls by twin-clouds odourous.
Twelve sphered tables, by silk seats inspher'd,
High as the level of a man's breast rear'd
On libbard's paws, upheld the heavy gold   185
Of cups and goblets, and the store thrice told
Of Ceres' horn, and, in huge vessels, wine
Come from the gloomy tun with merry shine.
Thus loaded with a feast the tables stood,
Each shrining in the midst the image of a God.   190

   When in an antichamber every guest
Had felt the cold full sponge to pleasure press'd,
By minist'ring slaves, upon his hands and feet,
And fragrant oils with ceremony meet
Pour'd on his hair, they all mov'd to the feast   195
In white robes, and themselves in order plac'd
Around the silken couches, wondering
Whence all this mighty cost and blaze of wealth could spring.

Soft went the music the soft air along,
While fluent Greek a vowel'd undersong   200
Kept up among the guests, discoursing low
At first, for scarcely was the wine at flow ;
But when the happy vintage touch'd their brains,
Louder they talk, and louder come the strains
Of powerful instruments :—the gorgeous dyes   205
The space, the splendour of the draperies,
The roof of awful richness, nectarous cheer,
Beautiful slaves, and Lamia's self, appear,
Now, when the wine has done its rosy deed,
And every soul from human trammels freed,   210
No more so strange ; for merry wine, sweet wine,
Will make Elysian shade not too fair, too divine.
Soon was God Bacchus at meridian height ;
Flush'd were their cheeks, and bright eyes double bright :
Garlands of every green, and every scent   215
From vales deflower'd, or forest-trees branch-rent,
In baskets of bright osier'd gold were brought
High as the handles heap'd, to suit the thought
Of every guest ; that each, as he did please,
Might fancy-fit his brows, silk-pillow'd at his ease.   220

What wreath for Lamia ?   What for Lycius ?
What for the sage, old Apollonius ?
Upon her aching forehead be there hung
The leaves of willow and of adder's tongue ;
And for the youth, quick, let us strip for him   225
The thyrsus, that his watching eyes may swim
Into forgetfulness ; and, for the sage,
Let spear-grass and the spiteful thistle wage
War on his temples.   Do not all charms fly
At the mere touch of cold philosophy ?   230
There was an awful rainbow once in heaven :
We know her woof, her texture ; she is given

In the dull catalogue of common things.
Philosophy will clip an Angel's wings,
Conquer all mysteries by rule and line,   235
Empty the haunted air, and gnomed mine—
Unweave a rainbow, as it erewhile made
The tender-person'd Lamia melt into a shade.

  By her glad Lycius sitting, in chief place,
Scarce saw in all the room another face,   240
Till, checking his love trance, a cup he took
Full brimm'd, and opposite sent forth a look
'Cross the broad table, to beseech a glance
From his old teacher's wrinkled countenance,
And pledged him.   The bald-head philosopher   245
Had fix'd his eye, without a twinkle or stir
Full on the alarmed beauty of the bride,
Brow-beating her fair form, and troubling her sweet pride.
Lycius then press'd her hand, with devout touch,
As pale it lay upon the rosy couch :   250
'Twas icy, and the cold ran through his veins ;
Then sudden it grew hot, and all the pains
Of an unnatural heat shot to his heart.
" Lamia, what means this ?   Wherefore dost thou start ?
Know'st thou that man ? "   Poor Lamia answer'd not.
He gaz'd into her eyes, and not a jot   256
Own'd they the lovelorn piteous appeal :
More, more he gaz'd : his human senses reel :
Some hungry spell that loveliness absorbs ;
There was no recognition in those orbs.   260
" Lamia ! " he cry'd—and no soft-ton'd reply.
The many heard, and the loud revelry
Grew hush ; the stately music no more breathes ;
The myrtle sicken'd in a thousand wreaths.
By faint degrees, voice, lute, and pleasure ceased ;   265
A deadly silence step by step increased,

Until it seem'd a horrid presence there,
And not a man but felt the terror in his hair.
" Lamia ! " he shriek'd ; and nothing but the shriek
With its sad echo did the silence break.   270
" Begone, foul dream ! " he cry'd, gazing again
In the bride's face, where now no azure vein
Wander'd on fair-spac'd temples ; no soft bloom
Misted the cheek ; no passion to illume
The deep-recessed vision :—all was blight ;   275
Lamia, no longer fair, there sat a deadly white.
" Shut, shut those juggling eyes, thou ruthless man !
Turn them aside, wretch ! or the righteous ban
Of all the Gods, whose dreadful images
Here represent their shadowy presences,   280
May pierce them on the sudden with the thorn
Of painful blindness ; leaving thee forlorn,
In trembling dotage to the feeblest fright
Of conscience, for their long offended might,
For all thine impious proud-heart sophistries,   285
Unlawful magic, and enticing lies.
Corinthians ! look upon that gray-beard wretch !
Mark how, possess'd, his lashless eyelids stretch
Around his demon eyes !   Corinthians, see !
My sweet bride withers at their potency."   290
" Fool ! " said the sophist, in an under-tone
Gruff with contempt ; which a death-nighing moan
From Lycius answer'd, as heart-struck and lost,
He sank supine beside the aching ghost.
" Fool ! Fool ! " repeated he, while his eyes still   295
Relented not, nor mov'd ; " from every ill
Of life have I preserv'd thee to this day,
And shall I see thee made a serpent's prey ? "
Then Lamia breath'd death breath ; the sophist's eye,
Like a sharp spear, went through her utterly,   300
Keen, cruel, perceant, stinging : she, as well

As her weak hand could any meaning tell,
Motion'd him to be silent ; vainly so,
He look'd and look'd again a level—No !
" A serpent ! " echoed he ; no sooner said,   305
Than with a frightful scream she vanished :
And Lycius' arms were empty of delight,
As were his limbs of life, from that same night.
On the high couch he lay !—his friends came round—
Supported him—no pulse, or breath they found,   310
And, in its marriage robe, the heavy body wound.

NOTES.

ISABELLA.

Isabella was intended for inclusion in a collection of tales from Boccaccio* to be versified by Keats's friend Reynolds, but Reynolds thought it too good to publish with the only two attempts he himself found time to complete. The poem was begun in February 1818 and finished before the end of April. It follows its source (*Decameron*, Day iv. Novel 5) closely as to facts, merely giving Isabella two brothers instead of three, providing the brothers with a mercenary motive for the murder, and transferring the scene of the story from Messina to Florence ; but Keats's treatment of the story is completely original.

The metre is the *ottava rima*, a favourite with Italian writers, used frequently by the Elizabethan poets and resuscitated about this time, notably by Lord Byron, who, however, used it for humorous purposes : it consists of eight iambic pentameters, rhyming *ab ab ab cc*. Keats manages his metre skilfully, avoiding monotony by change of pause rather than by variation of accent : apart from the frequent substitution of a trochee (*e.g. Gréw, líke*) for the iamb in the first foot, there is little departure from strict regularity—l. 62, where there is an extra short syllable, *bў ŭnwélcŏme*—is an exception.

But the great beauty of the poem undoubtedly lies not in the metre but in the narrative and the diction. The story is told simply and directly, and our sympathy is enlisted throughout—indeed, one captious critic, ignoring the distinction between a classic and a romantic poet, has complained that Keats occasionally in his sympathy with his heroine appeals to us in his own person instead of leaving the plain tale to have its own effect. The insight into character and feeling shown is indeed remarkable for so young a poet ; apart from the realistic detail of the first three stanzas—in which the youth of the poet was probably an advantage—stanzas xlvi. and xlvii. have been particularly praised, while the insane laughter of the distraught girl (stanza lxii.) adds a graphic and unexpected touch of horror and realism combined.

---

* Giovanni Boccaccio (1313-75) was the author of the great Italian collection of tales, the *Decameron*.

Here, too, though perhaps not so much as in *Hyperion* and *The Eve of St. Agnes*, Keats's wonderful picture-making power is evident : see, for instance, ll. 199-200, 213-15, 239, 298-304—Keats has imagined his characters and their surroundings so vividly that with his mind's eye he can see them more clearly and in greater detail than the common man can see objects which have a material existence.

The diction, again, though there are not quite so many magic phrases as in some other of his poems, has " every rift loaded with ore." Except for a very few prosaic colloquialisms which are the legacy of Leigh Hunt, and the repeated invocation of Melancholy, Music, and Melpomene in stanzas lv., lvi., and lxi., which, though beautiful in itself, is a thought too artificial for the simple tragedy of the theme, there is hardly a phrase which could be improved. Especially noteworthy is the lovely effect of the repetition in stanzas xi. and liii. and the concentrated poetry of such phrases as *lazar stairs* (l. 124), *torched mines* (l. 108), *Cut Mercy with a sharp knife to the bone* (l. 174), *Hope's accursed bands* (l. 230).

2. **palmer** : a pilgrim to the Holy Land who carried a palm-branch as a memento of his pilgrimage ; Lorenzo is a pilgrim to the Holy Land of love.

16. **She . . . same** : *i.e.* by inattentive stitching as she uttered his name.

21. **vespers** : "evening prayers."

32. **honeyless days** : "days without the sweetness of acknowledged love."

33. **untouch'd** : *i.e.* unkissed.

34. **within . . . domain** : "where it should have been rosy."

36. **cool** : a more poetical because a more exact and vivid word than the usual *soothe*.

39. **If looks . . . tears** : "if her looks mean that she loves me, I will dry her tears."

44. **ruddy tide** : *i.e.* of his blood which throbbed so fiercely (*puls'd*) that his decision melted and he could not speak.

46. **conceit** : "thought, imagination."

62. **fear** : "affright."

64. **shrive** : "confess."

70. **poesied . . . rhyme** : "made poetry by kissing hers," the two pair of lips corresponding to the two rhymes.

78. **honey'd dart** : Cupid, the god of love, is always represented as armed with bow and arrows, the wounds from which cause love.

88. **pleasure** : "find pleasure."

94. **in bright gold . . . read** : *i.e.* should be considered happy.

95. **Theseus' spouse** : Ariadne, daughter of Minos, who fell in love

with Theseus when he was sent to carry the tribute of the Athenians to a monster called the Minotaur, who lived in a labyrinth. She helped him to kill the monster and escape, and then fled with him ; he, however, deserted her on the island of Naxos. Tales of desertion, Keats implies, are truly sad, but most sorrowing lovers are really happy.

97. for . . . award : " as regards the usual upshot."

99. Dido : Dido, the Queen of Carthage, deserted by Aeneas, killed herself.

101-2. though . . . embalm'd : a reference to the fashion in which Lorenzo was buried, without coffin, shroud, or ceremony.

103 almsmen of spring bowers : " those who beg their living from the flowers of spring."

107. swelt : " toil, swelter."

108. torched : " lighted by torches."

109. quiver'd : " now quivering " : another suggestion is *once proud-quiver'd*—" once proudly bearing a quiver full of arrows."

112. rich-or'd . . . flood : " the gold washed down by the river."

113. Ceylon diver : *i.e.* the diver for pearls : the accent is on the first syllable of *Ceylon*, as in a passage of Dryden's *Annus Mirabilis*, which probably suggested some phrases in these lines.

124. lazar stairs : *i.e.* stairs on which lepers lay asking alms, the allusion being to the story of the Rich Man and Lazarus (St. Luke, xvi. 19-31, especially verse 20).

125-6. Because . . . years : " because they took more pleasure in their account-books ruled with red lines than in old Greek poems ? "

127-8. Why . . . proud : this absurd and feeble repetition is one of the few weak passages in the poem.

131-2. that land . . . beggar-spies : probably a reference to the Holy Land. pal'd : " fenced."

133-6. hawks . . . Malay : the brothers were ready to swoop like hawks upon the forest of masts, *i.e.* upon trading-vessels. They bore as easily as mules a load of money and the lies needed to gain it, snatched as quick as cat's paws at any unwary and open-hearted victim, and were fluent in the foreign languages most useful for commerce.

140. Hot Egypt's pest : probably " all the plagues of Egypt," with reference to Exodus vii.-xi.

146. forgiving boon : " the boon of forgiveness."

147. thy spicy myrtles : a reference to the Italian scenery in which Boccaccio lived.

150. ghittern : gittern or cittern, an instrument like a guitar ; Keats took the word from Chaucer.

155. assail : " attempt " ; Keats uses the verb as a noun.

159. **stead thee** : "benefit thee."

163. **unconfines** : "releases, discloses."

168. **To some . . . noble** : *i.e.* "to wed some great noble."

174. **Cut . . . bone** : "destroyed mercy, became merciless " : the metaphor is very vivid and peculiarly appropriate when applied to murderers.

183. **speculation** : "meditation."

184. **while . . . skies** : "before the day grows hot."

187-8. **ere the hot sun . . . eglantine** : "before the sun has dried up one of the drops of dew on the dog-rose, as if he were telling the beads of his rosary one by one."

189. **was wont** : "was accustomed to do."

195. **matin-song** : "morning song."

203. **fain** : strictly "glad," but here rather "hard put to it."

207. **Goodbye . . . back** : a feeble colloquialism which shows the influence of Leigh Hunt.

209. **their murder'd man** : rightly the most famous phrase in the poem.

211. **straiten'd** : "narrowed."

243. **single** : "with undivided love and allegiance."

246. **higher . . . zest** : *i.e.* passion and sorrow.

259. **dungeon climes** : "foreign countries which served as a prison to keep him from her."

262. **like . . . vale** : a reference to II. Chronicles, xxviii. 3 ; the smoke recalled to Ahaz his murder of his children.

268. **from . . . pall** : *i.e.* from death.

270. **from his cloudy hall** : "from the dim other-world of his belief to which he has almost gone," *i.e.* from death.

278. **lute** : *i.e.* notes soft like those of the lute.

279. **lorn** : "lost." **loamed** : "stopped with earth."

312. **in Humanity** : "because still forming part of humanity, still alive."

322. **left the atom darkness . . . turmoil** : "left the darkness, all composed of tiny particles, slowly whirling." Keats is probably thinking of the theory that everything is composed of atoms, a theory put forward in the *De Rerum Natura* of Lucretius (95 B.C.-52 B.C.).

325. **pillowy cleft** : "hollow in the pillow " : Keats himself in his illness often experienced such nights of wretchedness.

334. **school'd my infancy** : "taught me, who was inexperienced as a child."

339. **the clay** : *i.e.* the corpse.

347. champaign : " field."

352. The flint . . . head : see ll 298-9.

370. Her silk . . . phantasies : " she had embroidered fanciful patterns in purple silk."

380. locks of hoar : " grey hair " ; a peculiar use of *hoar* as a noun.

384. And . . . rave : an unexpectedly weak line, clearly due to the necessity of rhyming with *grave*.

385. wormy circumstance : " details of the grave."

388. plaining : " complaining, mourning."

393. Persean sword : the sword of Perseus, who cut off the head of Medusa, the gorgon, a monstrous maiden with serpents for hair, the sight of whose face turned the beholder to stone.

398. love impersonate : " love incarnate in human form," *i.e.* Lorenzo.

412. serpent-pipe : " pipe twisted like a serpent."

427. its peers . . . tufts · " the other plants of Basil." peers : " equals."

432. leafits : " leaflets " ; the form was used by Coleridge in the first edition of his *Nightingale*.

436. Lethean : " forgotten " ; the waters of the river Lethe in the underworld gave oblivion.

439. cypress : the cypress is symbolical of grief.

442. Melpomene : one of the nine Muses ; she presided over tragedy.

451. Baälites of pelf : worshippers of the Baal of money. Baal was the chief male divinity of the Phoenicians, and was also worshipped by the Canaanites. He appears to have been a sun-god.

453. elf : " person," simply.

465. sift : " examine closely."

467. chapel-shrift : " confession."

477. guerdon : " reward."

485. Well-a-way : " alas ! ", from the Old English wà là wà, *i.e* woe, lo ! woe.

493. the Pilgrim : *i.e.* any passing pilgrim.

THE EVE OF ST. AGNES.

The Eve of St. Agnes was written in 1819 ; it was begun in January, and it is pleasant to imagine that the date may have been St. Agnes' Eve itself—the 20th. The story is of Keats's own invention, founded upon the superstitions connected with the day : like many of our best narratives it has a very simple plot, so simple that the common man would think it incapable of arousing interest. But in Keats's hands it has become one of the most entrancing of English verse tales.

The narrative itself is well-sustained—there is no irrelevance, no digression, no intricate side-plot ; but these are negative virtues : in themselves they would not give the poem its fascination. What really attracts us is the series of wonderful pictures and fine phrases, the skilful contrast—in a word, the glamorous appeal to the eye and the ear. First we have a striking description of the cold and silent night, a study in black and frosty white : from this we pass to the "chambers ready with their pride," full of light and colour, sound and warmth, and then again to the quiet of Madeline's room. Where all is beautiful it is hard to pick out beauties, but the descriptions of the "carved angels" (stanza iv.), of Madeline in the glow of the moonlighted windows (stanzas xxiv. and xxv.), of Madeline asleep "in lap of legends old" perhaps linger in our memories more vividly than any others. The poem has all the brightness of a mediaeval illuminated manuscript, all the old-world charm of Spenser, whose stanza Keats has here used.

5. **Beadsman** : a man who prayed for the soul of others ; generally, as here, an almsman praying for the soul of his benefactor.

12. **meagre, barefoot, wan** : Keats uses elsewhere similar sets of three adjectives placed side by side so as to give cumulative effect ; he probably learnt the device from Chatterton, the boy-poet (1752-70).

15. **black purgatorial rails** : the rails are regarded as cramping in the effigies, thus inflicting the pains of purgatory : as Leigh Hunt pointed out, the idea is reminiscent of a passage in the *Purgatorio* of the great Italian poet Dante (1265-1321), which Keats had read in translation : he adds "the very colour of the rails is made to . . . shadow forth the gloom of the punishment."

16. **dumb orat'ries** : *dumb* is a transferred epithet ; in meaning, it is applicable only to *knights, ladies.*

21. **Flatter'd to tears** : the music moved the old man to tears of hope and self-pity ; he flattered himself that a brighter fate would now be his lot.

26. **for his soul's reprieve** : " to save his soul from future torment."

29. **And . . . fro** : " and he happened to hear it because many a door was open in consequence of the hurried coming and going."

49. **honey'd** : " sweet," a favourite word with Keats.

51. **As** : " for instance."

52. **couch supine** : " lay flat."

53. **require** : " ask."

54. After this line the manuscript in the British Museum has another stanza to the effect that the lover would bring delicious food and soft music—thus accounting for Porphyrio's otherwise meaningless behaviour later in providing food which Madeline was not expected to eat.

61. **not . . . saw not** : " not because his ardour was frozen by a disdainful glance from Madeline but because she did not see him."

64. **regardless** : " unseeing."

70. **Hoodwink'd . . . fancy** : *i.e.* cheated of a sense of her surroundings by her imagination, that " deceiving elf." **amort** : " dead to all around."

71. **St. Agnes . . . unshorn** : the name Agnes being connected with the Latin *agnus*, " a lamb," two lambs were brought to Mass on St. Agnes' day and offered during the chanting of the *Agnus Dei* (" O Lamb of God, who takest away the sins of the world," etc.). Their wool was afterwards clipped and woven by the nuns. See ll. 115-18.

77. **Buttress'd from moonlight** : *i.e.* protected by a buttress from the moonlight, which would have disclosed his presence.

84. **his heart . . . citadel** : " his heart in which, as in a fortress, love feverishly keeps guard."

90. **beldame** : literally, *fair dame* ; but used only of old hags.

105. **gossip** : " friend," literally " one related in God, *i.e.* by baptism ; a sponsor."

120. **hold . . . sieve** : witches were credited with the ability to make a sieve non-porous : cp. *Macbeth*, I. iii. 8, " But in a sieve I'll thither sail."

124-5. **my lady . . . deceive** : *i.e.* this very night Madeline is trying to conjure up a vision ; may the good angels send her a dream which she may mistake for a miracle.

126. **mickle** : " much."

127. **moon** : *i.e.* " moonlight," the moon being personified so as to admit of the beautiful epithet *languid.*

133. **brook** : " check, restrain," a misuse of the word, which means *use, enjoy,* or *endure.*

155. **churchyard thing** : " creature only fit to be buried."

158. **plaining** : " complaining, lamenting."

165. **closet** : " cupboard."

168. **While . . . coverlet** : " while in her dreams she saw legions of fairies walking upon her bed."

171. **Since . . . debt** : Merlin was the son of a demon and consequently had to return to hell, Vivian working upon him one of his own spells.

173. **cates** : " dainties, delicacies " ; cp. *catering.*

174. **tambour frame** : " embroidery frame."

185. **From . . . espial** : " from fear that Porphyro might be spied in the half-dark."

192. **St. Agnes' charmed maid** : " a maid working St. Agnes's charms."

193. **mission'd** : " sent upon a mission."

198. **fray'd** : " frightened."

204. **But . . . voluble** : *i.e.* but her heart, beating quickly, told her heart (*i e.* told her) how agitated she was.

213. **deep-damask'd** : " richly embroidered."

215. **emblazonings** : " heraldic decorations."

216. **scutcheon** : " a shield on which the heraldic arms of a family are emblazoned."

218. **gules** : the heraldic term for *red.*

237. **poppied** : poppies, since they contain opium, are an emblem of sleep.

238. **soul fatigued away** : the soul is conceived as leaving the body during sleep.

241. **Clasp'd . . . pray** : *i.e.* clasped closely and lovingly, since a missal or prayer-book would be doubly precious in a pagan land. **swart Paynims** : " dark pagans."

246-7. **if it . . . tenderness** : *i.e.* to hear when her breathing took the slow regularity which showed she was asleep.

253. **faded moon** : *i.e.* setting moon.

257. **Morphean amulet** : " charm to give sleep " so that the noise should not wake Madeline before the table was prepared : Morpheus was the god of sleep.

266. **soother** : " more soothing."

267. **lucent** : " reflecting or giving out light."   **tinct** : " coloured."

277. **eremite** : " hermit "

286. **redeem** : " bring back " : it seemed as if he could never break the spell which kept Madeline asleep.

288. **So . . . phantasies** : "so he mused for a time, caught in a web of fancies." **woofed** : "woven."

292. **La belle dame sans mercy** : "the merciless fair lady"; the reference shows Keats's preoccupation with the subject which he was later to treat in his own fine poem with this title : the mediaeval poem extant with this title is an unpoetic and monotonous dialogue between a lover and his disdainful mistress. It was in Provence that the famous mediaeval school of love-poetry had its origin.

296. **affrayed** : "frightened."

322. **Solution** : "intermingling."

325. **flaw-blown** : "wind-blown"; a flaw is a gust of wind.

333. **unpruned** : "ruffled, untrimmed."

336. **heart . . . dy'd** : heart-shaped because his heart is hers, and flushed with love.

344. **haggard seeming** : "wretched appearance"; the adjective *haggard* is one of Keats's strikingly poetic epithets.

346. **bloated wassailers** : this and the following stanzas probably contain reminiscences of *Hamlet* and *Macbeth*—the fondness of the "bloat king" Claudius for "Rhenish" in the first play and the drunken Porter in the second.

349. **Rhenish** : *i.e.* Rhenish wine.

353. **sleeping dragons** : *i.e.* her kinsmen, the foes of Porphyro.

357. **chain-droop'd** : "hanging from a chain."

358. **arras** : "tapestry."

366. **his . . . owns** : "his wise eye recognises Madeline as a member of the household," so that he makes no sound.

377. **aves** : prayers in honour of the Virgin Mary—"Ave Maria, gratia plena."—"Hail, Mary! full of grace."

LAMIA.

Lamia, written in 1819, was the last long poem which Keats finished and published : it shows Keats at his best in sheer narrative power. Before writing the poem, he made a careful study of the work of Dryden, and he here uses the heroic couplet first perfected by that poet. Like Dryden, he varies his metre by the use of alexandrines (lines with six iambic feet instead of five), like Dryden he gains a force and sweep of rhythm and an easy stride of narrative by shifting the pause in the line and by a skilful mixture of lines which end with the sense and " run-on lines," where the sense is carried on to the next line : such a couplet, for instance as :

> " For somewhere in that sacred island dwelt
> A nymph, to whom all hoofed satyrs knelt "

might have been written by Dryden himself except for the " picture-word " *hoofed*.

The source of his story Keats gave himself in a footnote to his poem :—

" Philostratus, in his fourth book *de Vita Apollonii*, hath a memorable instance of this kind, which I may not omit, of one Menippus Lycius, a young man twenty-five years of age, that going betwixt Cenchreas and Corinth, met such a phantasm in the habit of a fair gentlewoman, which taking him by the hand, carried him home to her house, in the suburbs of Corinth, and told him she was a Phoenician by birth, and if he would tarry with her, he should hear her sing and play, and drink such wine as never any drank, and no man should molest him ; but she, being fair and lovely, would live and die with him, that was fair and lovely to behold. The young man, a philosopher, otherwise staid and discreet, able to moderate his passions, though not this of love, tarried with her a while to his great content, and at last married her, to whose wedding, amongst other guests, came Apollonius ; who, by some probable conjectures, found her out to be a serpent, a lamia ; and that all her furniture was, like Tantalus' gold, described by Homer, no substance but mere illusions. When she saw herself descried, she wept, and desired Apollonius to be silent, but he would not be moved, and thereupon she, plate, house, and all that was in it, vanished in an instant :

many thousands took notice of this fact, for it was done in the midst of Greece."

Burton's "Anatomy of Melancholy." Part 3. Sect. 2. Memb. 1. Subs. 1.

And it is interesting to see how much the poetic imagination can make of the merest hint. "All her furniture was, like Tantalus' gold . . . no substance, but mere illusions," for instance, provides all Keats's "authority" for ll. 379-93 of Part I., and ll. 117-41 and 173-208 of Part II., perhaps the most splendid passages in the poem.

But it is not merely these luxurious beauties that appeal to us ; not merely the incidental nature-touches such as "About a young bird's flutter from a wood " ; it is Lamia herself and her piteous fate. By all the laws of morality we ought to rejoice at the youth's escape from the serpent-woman, but Keats enlists all our sympathy on behalf of the two lovers. Even illusion, he seems to say, is better than hard fact, if only it is beautiful. Perhaps we have here a revelation of his own feeling—the beauty which he saw in everything, the poetry which he wrote, what was it after all to the scientific mind but illusion and play-acting ? Keats is protesting against the narrowing of reason to mean mere logical reasoning, and against the gross materialism and the increasing ugliness of his age quite as much as against the eternal opposition of cynical old age to the romantic love-follies of youth.

PART I.

2. **Nymph and Satyr** : the nymphs were in classical mythology goddesses of mountains, lakes, woods, etc. ; satyrs were beings of the woods, with pointed ears, two small horns and a tail.

3. **Oberon** : the fairy king.

5. **the Dryads and the Fauns** : the Dryads were nymphs of the trees ; fauns were woodland beings, half-man, half-goat.

7. **ever-smitten Hermes** : Mercury, the messenger of the gods, ever in love : *smitten* in this sense is a vulgar colloquialism which the mature Keats would certainly not have used.

9. **Olympus** : the mountain of Thessaly in Greece on the top of which the gods were believed to live. **light** : "silently, unperceived."

10. **Jove** : Zeus, the chief of the gods, Hermes' " great summoner."

15. **Tritons** : sea-deities, the top half of which was man, while below the waist they were fish.

16. **wither'd** : because out of their native water.

19. **Muse** : the nine Muses presided over poetry, music, the arts and sciences.

23. **winged heels** : Hermes is always represented with wings at his ankles.

38. **wreathed tomb** : *i.e.* the snake's twisted body.

46. **cirque-couchant** : "lying curled in a circle."

47. **gordian** : "intricate, twisted," in reference to the knot which the Phrygian king Gordius tied in his harness and which Alexander cut with his sword, an oracle having declared that whoever loosened the knot would rule over all Asia.

49. **pard** : "leopard."

55. **penanc'd lady elf** : "fairy undergoing penance."

57. **wannish** : "pale."

58. **Ariadne's tiar** : the crown of Ariadne, who, after helping Theseus to escape from the labyrinth of the monster Minotaur, was deserted by him at Naxos but wedded by Dionysus, the god of wine, who placed among the stars the crown which he gave her at her wedding.

63. **Proserpine . . . Silician air** : Proserpine, daughter of Ceres, was gathering flowers in Sicily when Pluto, the god of the infernal regions, carried her off to be his queen.

67. **stoop'd falcon** : "falcon hovering in readiness for the final swoop."

74. **Apollo** : the god of the sun, of poetry, and of song; also known as Phoebus (see l. 78).

81. **star of Lethe** : it was the duty of Hermes to lead the souls of the dead to the river Lethe in the underworld, whose waters gave oblivion.

85. **Possess . . . fled** : "thou shalt have whatever joy thou choosest if thou tellest me where my nymph is fled."

92. **brilliance feminine** : a rather tasteless abstraction, though probably due to Miltonic influence.

103. **blear'd Silenus** : Silenus, one of the satyrs, was a drunken, jovial, fat old man. **sights** : "glances."

104. **Pale grew her immortality** : an admirably compressed phrase for "pale grew the immortal nymph," combined with a suggestion that her very immortality was growing faint.

107. **weird** : two syllables.

114. **psalterian** : *i.e.* melodious as the notes of the psaltery, an ancient Jewish stringed instrument.

115. **Circean** : Circe was an enchantress who turned men into animals.

116. **live damask** : "vivid red."

131. **printless verdure** : "greensward unmarked by footprints."

133. **lythe Caducean charm** : the spell of his slender caduceus or wand round which were twined two serpents.

138. **fearful** : " full of fear."

148. **besprent** : " sprinkled."

155. **Volcanian** : " as from a volcano " ; see l. 157.

156. **milder-mooned** : see l. 136.

158. **brede** : " embroidery," hence " ornamentation."

163. **rubious-argent** : reddish silver.

167. **luting** : " sounding like a lute."

174. **Cenchreas** : Cenchreae was the East harbour of Corinth ; *Cleonae* (l. 179) was a town on the road from Corinth to Argos.

182. **passioned** : " gave way to passion, grief."

188. **Spread . . . minstrelsy** : " danced in a green skirt to the minstrels' music."

191. **sciential . . . pain** : " full of knowledge sufficient to disentangle joy from the pain into which it so easily changes."

193-4. **estrange . . . counterchange** : " make the points where they meet strangers to each other (*i.e.* keep them apart), and prevent the interchange between them which can so quickly take place."

195. **Intrigue . . . chaos** : " entangle the fair-seeming confusion of joy and pain and place in their proper places even those atoms of each feeling whose nature is most obscure."

198. **unshent** : " unharmed."

206. **Elysium:** part of the lower world, the abode of the spirits of the Blessed.

207. **Nereids** : sea-nymphs, sisters of Thetis, and daughters of Nereus and Doris.

209. **Bacchus** : the god of wine.

210. **glutinous pine** : an allusion to the pitchy nature of the pine tree.

211. **Pluto** : the god of the underworld. **palatine** : invested with royal privileges.

212. **Mulciber's . . . line** : the alexandrine here echoes the sense. **Mulciber** : a surname of Vulcan, the god of fire, and the artist of the gods : he made all the Olympian palaces. **piazzian** : connected with *piazza*—a walk under a roof supported by pillars.

217. **envious race** : " race of those anxious for victory and envious of others' success.

219. **swooning** : all Keats's lovers swoon readily ; perhaps his own ill-health made the idea of swooning come more readily to him than to the normal man.

220. **moth-time** : " the time when moths come forth "—an exquisite phrase.

225. **Egina** : a rocky island in a bay of the Aegean Sea.

229. **better'd his desire** : " gave him a better boon than he had asked."

230. made retire from : "retired from, left."

235-6. His . . . shades : his fancy strayed and, like reason, lost itself in the doubtful philosophic speculations of Plato (429-347 B.C.), the great disciple of Socrates, who taught in the shady groves of Athens.

240. neighbour'd : "near, like a neighbour."

244. syllabling : "speaking"; the word has four syllables.

246. be : *i.e.* "let there be."

248. But Orpheus-like . . . Eurydice : *i.e.* like one devoured by love. Eurydice having died, her husband Orpheus descended to the underworld, and by his wonderful harping gained permission for Eurydice to follow him back to the world above, provided he did not look at her until they regained daylight. On the way back, however, he could not refrain from looking round at her, and thus lost her for ever.

256. she saw . . . sure : "she saw that he was fast caught in the bonds of love."

260. To thy . . . obey : "thy streams will obey thee even if thou commandest when far away from them."

265. Pleiad : the Pleiades were the daughters of Atlas and Pleione; they were metamorphosed into doves and placed among the stars.

275. To . . . home : "to blunt my memory of my delicate home"; *nice* is probably another transferred epithet : otherwise *nice* may be taken as *exact, precise.*

293. amenity : "pleasure, delight."

313-14. Days . . . love : "days as happy as money could provide for one without love."

317. Venus : the goddess of love; she fell in love with Adonis, who was killed by a boar : his death and return to life were celebrated in annual festivals; hence *Adonian feast* (l. 320).

329. Peris : in Persian mythology a fairy, a descendant of a fallen spirit excluded from Paradise.

330. such a treat : a touch of vulgar colloquialism, probably due to the influence of Leigh Hunt : so, too, *half a fright* in l. 335 : the whole of this passage (330-9) is in poor taste.

333. Pyrrha's pebbles : according to classical mythology there was a flood in which all except Deucalion and Pyrrha were destroyed : Pyrrha created a fresh race by throwing over her shoulders stones which changed into women; in the same way Deucalion created men.

345. made by a spell the triple . . . paces : "by magic made the distance, three leagues, shrink into a few steps." **surmised** : this elliptically qualifies the idea in the whole preceding sentence—Lycius did not guess what she had done.

347. comprized : " absorbed."

359. their : this refers to *men* and *women* in l. 355.

381. slabbed : " covered with slabs of stone."

386. Aeolian : " made by the wind Aeolus."

394. but : " except that." flitter-winged : either " bat-winged " and hence " gloomy," *flittermouse* meaning *bat*; or else " fluttering from subject to subject " : the word appears to be coined by Keats.

PART II.

6. non-elect : " those who are not love's chosen " ; the phrase originates in the Calvinistic theological doctrine that certain people are elect or chosen by God for salvation, the rest of mankind being damned.

8. given . . . a fresh frown : frowned upon or disputed the moral that love in a palace is torment.

9. clench'd it quite : " completely confirmed it."

10. hiss : with anger ; in view of Lamia's origin, the word is here strikingly appropriate.

26. slope : " sloping," a word borrowed by Keats from Milton.

35. so arguing : qualifying *this*.

36. empery : " empire, rule."

39. That . . . bell : " that even a moment's reflection tolls the knell (*i.e.* means the death) of passion."

47. Where . . . paradise : the reference is of course to the reflection of his face in miniature in her eyes.

48. silver planet : " star."

53. labyrinth : " hide, as in a labyrinth."

57-60. What mortal hath a prize which may make other men abashed and confused with envy and yet keeps it hid from sight ?

76. sanguineous : " flushed with angry blood."

81. burnt : *i.e.* with love.

90. cited earth : probably *cited* is a transferred epithet meaning " who should be summoned," and belongs to *friends or kinsfolk*.

98. list : " please."

107. shut : " close," the word in this connection is Milton's.

122-3. The faery-roof was perhaps supported only by music.

136. mission'd : " sent."

137. fretted : " ornamented."

141. And . . . intricacies : " and interwove small designs with the large ones."

142. faded at self-will : " departed, to satisfy her own wish, from the crowded haunt of men ; shut herself up in solitude."

146. **gossip** : " friendly " ; originally one related in God, *i.e.* a sponsor.

155. **demesne** : " dominion."

160. **daft** : " baffled."

172. **sophist** : the Greek sophists taught philosophy and rhetoric ; from the tendency of some to quibbling our modern meaning of the word—captious and insincere reasoner—is derived. **spleen** : the spleen was formerly thought to be the seat of anger.

185. **libbard** : " leopard."

187. **Ceres** : the goddess of earth and the protectress of agriculture (cp. *cereal*). **horn** : " horn of plenty, cornucopia."

190. **shrining** : " holding as in a shrine."

200. **While . . . undersong** : *i.e.* the guests were fluently talking Greek, a language full of sonorous vowels.

207. **nectareous cheer** : " food and drink tasting like nectar, the wondrous drink of the gods."

213. **Soon . . . height** : *i.e.* soon they had drunk deeply. **Bacchus** : the god of wine. **meridian height** : mid-day height, *i.e.* the highest point.

220. **fancy-fit** : " fit according to his fancy."

224. **willow** : symbol of desertion and unrequited love. **adder's tongue** : to recall her serpent origin.

226. **thyrsus** : a staff entwined with ivy and vine leaves and grapes, with a cone at the top, carried at the festivals of Bacchus.

238. **spear-grass** : long, stiff grass : both this and the prickly thistle inflict pain.

229-38. **Do not . . . shade** : it is reported that Keats and Lamb at one of the meetings at Haydon's house, agreed that Sir Isaac Newton, the great scientist, " had destroyed all the poetry of the rainbow, by reducing it to the prismatic colours."

236. **gnomed** : " filled with gnomes " ; it was supposed that gnomes worked the metals underground.

274-5. **no passion . . . vision** : " no passion lighted her eyes, deep-sunk in her head."

288. **possess'd** : *i.e.* possessed by an evil spirit.

299. **breath'd death breath** : " drew her last breath as a woman."

301. **perceant** : " piercing."

PRINTED AT THE BURLINGTON PRESS, FOXTON, NEAR CAMBRIDGE, ENGLAND.

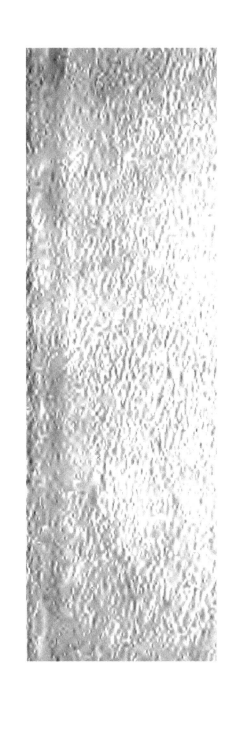

Lightning Source UK Ltd.
Milton Keynes UK
UKHW021851121222
413832UK00005B/109